VOLUME ONE

ADVANCING PSYCHOLOGICAL SCIENCE

ADVANCING PSYCHOLOGICAL SCIENCE

Volume 1: Philosophies, Methods, and Approaches

Volume 2: Research in Perception, Learning, and Conflict

Volume 3: Research in Developmental, Personality, and Social Psychology

EDITED BY

Fillmore H. Sanford

E. John Capaldi

THE UNIVERSITY OF TEXAS

PHILOSOPHIES, METHODS, AND APPROACHES

WADSWORTH PUBLISHING COMPANY, INC.
Belmont, California

FIRST PRINTING, MARCH 1964
SECOND PRINTING, JULY 1964

L.C. Cat. Card No.: 64–15484

Printed in the United States of America

PREFACE

Psychology teachers have many different aspirations for their undergraduate courses, and almost every teacher has his own strategy for making his course a rewarding experience for his students. Many teachers feel that a book of readings can add a significant dimension of meaning to regular courses, and these teachers will surely agree that the readings should supply something that the texts do not. Not all teachers see eye to eye, at the level of specifics, about the functions a readings book can serve, nor do they agree on what kinds of materials should be included in such an adjunct to a standard text. But all will give ready assent to the general proposition that a book of readings should add to the student's depth of understanding and increase his appreciation of the field of psychology. In preparing this series of readings books, the editors began with this one widely shared and relatively abstract aspiration and searched the literature for materials that they deemed likely to contribute to the depth and fullness of the student's experience as he studies the science of psychology.

A number of interlocking strategies guided the selection and arrangement of the materials. There was a strategy of packaging. Since not all teachers necessarily wish to assign all the material included in the lengthier books of readings, we thought it useful—and perhaps considerate of the student's book budget—to divide our selections into three smaller units, each constituting a coherent array of materials. Such a division will allow the individual teacher the choice of assigning those readings he feels he needs in order to supplement most meaningfully the combination of himself and the text he uses, or of assigning all three volumes if he wishes.

We felt also that there were three important ways in which properly selected readings can supplement texts and add to the richness of the student's experience. First, we believe it will be valuable for the student to see the science of psychology in context, as it exists among other scientific disciplines, and to see all the scientific disciplines—the whole scientific enterprise—in the more general context of man's various attempts to make sense out of the world he lives in. Volume 1 of this series is our attempt to do something about that belief. Therefore, it begins with a consideration of science in general, then works its way toward an appreciation of psychology as a scientific discipline.

Second, we felt that the student could neither fully understand nor properly appreciate psychology without digging deeply into at least a few substantive areas of concern. So we left the strategy of comprehensiveness to the textbooks, and selected materials for Volumes 2 and 3 that stay with a single topic long enough and explore it in enough different ways to give the student, if he seeks it, some knowledge-in-depth in selected areas of psychological research. There is no attempt to be either representative or comprehensive. There is instead an attempt to expose the student as fully as possible to a limited number of significant psychological problems.

Third, we felt strongly that students would not only profit by but perhaps also enjoy an intimate exposure to the intellectual adventure involved in the actual gathering of psychological knowledge. To implement this conviction, we chose materials that take the student relatively far—perhaps precipitously—into matters of methods. And by methods, we mean not only the bright gimmicks and gadgets used in experimentation, but the intellectual methods employed in the stating and testing of hypotheses. Also—a consideration we thought very important—we wanted the student to see and appreciate the cumulative process of science. So we began by searching for early articles that stated hypotheses that subsequently led to a substantial amount of research. Then we sampled the relevant literature in order to follow the scientific fate of the original hypotheses, and to reveal at least some of the ways in which that fate, through research, unfolds. Perhaps we tended to select articles generally favorable to the original hypotheses, as we did not want to produce too much cognitive strain. But we did put in some troubles and dissonances: we would not be presenting the reality of psychological research had we not, and to us there are obvious advantages in showing difficulties and puzzles as well as victories.

Although we try in various ways to help the student grasp the material we give him, the books, particularly the last two, may still be difficult reading. We are of two minds about that. Psychology is a difficult subject, we say, and the sooner the student knows it the better. Psychology is no longer, if it ever was, in the realm of codified and monosyllabic common sense. Psychology is not a simple discipline; but we still should not foist upon the student material that is forbiddingly difficult. Therefore, we hope that our introductory and interstitial material, together with the glossaries, will help reduce unnecessary and pointless difficulties. If these efforts are not enough, we comfort ourselves with the knowledge that the teacher is there to help, in ways no editor or text writer can aspire to.

We wish to express our appreciation here, as we have done in correspondence, to those instructors in various colleges and universities who gave us such willing and, in our eyes, such perceptive advice about the best functions for such volumes. We hope we have succeeded at least reasonably well in translating their ideas into usable books.

We have gratitude also, of a very special kind, for those psychologists whose works of research and scholarship are presented in this series. We hope we have represented them well, and that the appearance here of the results of their efforts will, in the long run, contribute —in a way that they themselves will approve—to the advancement of the discipline to which they have committed their creative efforts.

Finally, we wish to thank Mr. Hugh Poynor and Miss Willie O'Berry, who were asked to go one mile but went two in shepherding this project into print.

F. H. S.
E. J. C.

CONTENTS

INTRODUCTION

Psychology as a science exists in a human, cultural, intellectual, and historical context. It is the general purpose of this book to facilitate the appreciation of psychology in its context, a context shared at least partially with all other sciences and to some extent with any of man's attempts to understand the world and his own place in it.

Science in general may be viewed from many angles and given multiple definitions. It may, for example, be dealt with as if it were a body of knowledge, a highly evolved method of obtaining knowledge, a general attitude toward the solution of problems, or as a general philosophy of knowledge or of life itself. However one may approach the matter, there is no denying that science is a human endeavor forwarded by human beings. And it is clear that the human beings who forward it are not only subject to all the ills that flesh is heir to, but that they are also capable of rising to marvelous heights of creativity. They are human beings who as individuals and as a group are products of a cultural and a psychological history. They are human beings who now exist in a social and cultural setting, a setting that sometimes reveres, sometimes reviles, their work. And scientists are individuals who seek out one another, compare notes, exchange challenges, test one another's ideas, and contribute to the advancement of their common interest. Once a number of such individuals direct their curiosity to the same kind of problem, they begin to evolve methods and devices that are particularly adapted for the unraveling of the special kinds of puzzles they commonly confront. When a set of workable methods focused on one problem area becomes established, knowledge begins to accumulate. Scientists then speak the same language to one another, write to one another, take young people under their intellectual wings in order to train them properly in the ways of that particular discipline.

The first purpose of this book is to present some views—hopefully, revealing and cumulatively enlightening views—of science as a human endeavor, as a human endeavor with a history, as one of the various human approaches to the solution of some of the problems man poses for himself, and as a general set of linguistic and mathematical skills that human beings learn and use in the creation of scientific certitudes. The second purpose, advanced in the later sections of the book, is to regard psychological scientists and their science against the general human and historical background presented in the first part.

Most introductory texts in psychology, and most introductory courses also, pay considerable attention to matters of scientific method and to topics which fall in the area of the philosophy of science. Students often ask why psychologists should be so concerned with philosophy and method while physicists or chemists or biologists rarely bother with such matters. There are a number of reasons why this is so. Twenty or thirty years ago, psychologists were somewhat defensive in their emphasis on matters of scientific method. They needed the help of some of the larger minds in the philosophical field to demonstrate beyond a shadow of doubt that psychology was indeed scientific in nature. So every psychology course, introductory or otherwise, usually began with two or three lectures designed to show how truly scientific is the study of psychology, and how improper it was for the psychology department to be so unprestigiously housed in the attic or in the basement of the worst building on campus. At that time, too, it was highly fashionable for every graduate student in psychology to take not only a number of methodology courses, but also at least one course in the philosophy of science. In recent years, psychology has been accorded considerable respectability in housing and other symbols of acceptance, and there is little or no need for defensiveness or for vigorous protestations of scientific worth. But the emphasis on method and philosophy remains, in both graduate and undergraduate psychology curricula: what was born of defense has been functional in its own right and so has stayed alive.

It is probably true that psychologists maintain a uniquely keen interest in the philosophy and methods of science because matters of epistemology and method are basically matters of psychological process; they are matters of sensing, of perceiving, and of conceptualizing the world. Psychology, since its inception, has been concerned with these, the ways in which the human organism can know the world. So, in substantive terms, this core of psychology—and the core still receives a very great deal of research attention—is a core also of all science. And this will remain so; for scientific operations can occur only when a human being can sense, can perceive, and can conceive his world; only when he can ply these psychological operations in and upon his world can he make meaningful declarative sentences about it.

An illustration can be found in the science exhibit at the Seattle World's Fair of 1962, where visitors were exposed to demonstrations both of ordinary perceptual processes and of perceptual illusions before they were shown demonstrations in any substantive area of science. For psychology, perception is a problem. For all sciences, perception is the beginning of knowledge.

Many instructors argue also that undergraduate courses in psychology offer the student a unique opportunity to develop an intimate and truly functional grasp of scientific method. Although the nonphysicist or nonchemist will encounter few daily problems to which his practiced laboratory skills are applicable, the nonpsychologist will experience manifold problem situations to which the basic methods of psychology are relevant. The research skills and the attitudinal approaches of the research psychologist have a transferability about them; they involve general principles and general procedures which, once learned, can be applied to a wide variety of nonlaboratory problems. We need not delve into the reasons for this; but the case clearly can be made that there is a great human value in the addition of any increment to one's ability to perceive accurately and objectively, to scale or order his perceptions precisely, to apply concepts and categorizations with insight, or to infer with scientific justification.

1

SCIENCE IS A HUMAN ENDEAVOR

Whether the activity of scientists is the naturalistic observation of animals in the forest, the highly instrumented conduct of laboratory experiments, or the creative assembly of many apparently isolated and unrelated facts into the eloquent coherence of a theory, that activity is a human activity, carried on by extraordinarily persistent individuals who show, upon occasion, a seemingly wondrous capacity to create Einsteinian surprises. But individual scientists also possess human fallibility. Science as a human endeavor can be appreciated fully only if we see and consider not only the inventiveness of those who ply it but also their fallibilities both as individuals and as members of somewhat less than perfect social organizations.

We obviously cannot document all the human attributes of science and of scientists here. We focus, then, upon the human fallibilities of scientists; because many of the methods and attitudes that characterize the scientist at work—perhaps particularly the psychological scientist at work—are methods and attitudes that have developed from a recognition of human fallibilities and from creative efforts to contain and control the human proneness to err, err both in observation and in interpretation.

One of history's most remarkable treatises on the nature and the functioning of fallibility in the human observer was written more than three hundred years ago by Francis Bacon in his *Novum Organum*. Bacon's paragraphs on "The Four Idols," often cited and quoted—and sometimes misinterpreted—in other than scientific contexts, may be regarded not only as a commentary on scientific objectivity and the human failures to achieve it, but as essays about human cognition and the factors that contribute to errors in perceiving and conceiving external events.

THE FOUR IDOLS*

Francis Bacon

xxxviii

The idols and false notions which are now in possession of the human understanding, and have taken deep root therein, not only so beset men's minds that truth can hardly find entrance, but even after entrance obtained, they will again in the very instauration [institution] of the sciences meet and trouble us, unless men being forewarned of the danger fortify themselves as far as may be against their assaults.

xxxix

There are four classes of Idols which beset men's minds. To these for distinction's sake I have assigned names,—calling the first class *Idols of the Tribe;* the second, *Idols of the Cave;* the third, *Idols of the Market-place;* the fourth, *Idols of the Theatre.*

xl

The formation of ideas and axioms by true induction is no doubt the proper remedy to be applied for the keeping off and clearing away of idols. To point them out, however, is of great use; for the doctrine of Idols is to the Interpretation of Nature what the doctrine of the refutation of Sophisms is to common Logic.

xli

The Idols of the Tribe have their foundation in human nature itself, and in the tribe or race of men. For it is a false assertion that the sense of man is the measure of things. On the contrary, all perceptions as well of the sense as of the mind are according to the measure of the individual and not according to the measure of the universe. And the human understanding is like a false mirror, which, receiving rays irregularly, distorts and discolours the nature of things by mingling its own nature with it.

* Excerpted from Francis Bacon, "Novum Organum" (1620), in James Spedding, R. L. Ellis, and D. D. Heath (Eds.), *The Works of Francis Bacon.* London: Longman and Company, 1857–74.

xlii

The Idols of the Cave are the idols of the individual man. For everyone (besides the errors common to human nature in general) has a cave or den of his own, which refracts and discolours the light of nature; owing either to his own proper and peculiar nature; or to his education and conversation with others; or to the reading of books, and the authority of those whom he esteems and admires; or to the differences of impressions, accordingly as they take place in a mind preoccupied and predisposed or in a mind indifferent and settled; or the like. So that the spirit of man (according as it is meted out to different individuals) is in fact a thing variable and full of perturbation, and governed as it were by chance. Whence it was well observed by Heraclitus that men looked for sciences in their own lesser worlds, and not in the greater or common world.

xliii

There are also Idols formed by the intercourse and association of men with each other, which I call Idols of the Market-place, on account of the commerce and consort of men there. For it is by discourse that men associate; and words are imposed according to the apprehension of the vulgar. And therefore the ill and unfit choice of words wonderfully obstructs the understanding. Nor do the definitions or explanations wherewith in some things learned men are wont to guard and defend themselves, by any means set the matter right. But words plainly force and overrule the understanding, and throw all into confusion, and lead men away into numberless empty controversies and idle fancies.

xliv

Lastly, there are Idols which have immigrated into men's minds from the various dogmas of philosophies, and also from wrong laws of demonstration. These I call Idols of the Theatre; because in my judgment all the received systems are but so many stageplays, representing worlds of their own creation after an unreal and scenic fashion. Nor is it only of the systems now in vogue, or only of the ancient sects and philosophies, that I speak: for many more plays of the same kind may yet be composed and in like artificial manner set forth; seeing that errors the most widely different have nevertheless causes for the most part alike. Neither again do I mean this only of entire systems, but also of many principles and axioms in science, which by tradition, credulity, and negligence have come to be received.

But of these several kinds of Idols I must speak more largely and exactly, that the understanding may be duly cautioned.

xlv

The human understanding is of its own nature prone to suppose the existence of more order and regularity in the world than it finds. And though there be many things in nature which are singular and unmatched, yet it devises for them parallels and conjugates and relatives which do not exist. Hence the fiction that all celestial bodies move in perfect circles; spirals and dragons being (except in name) utterly rejected. Hence too the element of Fire with its orb is brought in, to make up the square with the other three which the sense perceives. Hence also the ratio of density of the so-called elements is arbitrarily fixed at ten to one. And so on of other dreams. And these fancies affect not dogmas only, but simple notions also.

xlvi

The human understanding when it has once adopted an opinion (either as being the received opinion or as being agreeable to itself) draws all things else to support and agree with it. And though there be a greater number and weight of instances to be found on the other side, yet these it either neglects and despises, or else by some distinction sets aside and rejects; in order that by this great and pernicious predetermination the authority of its former conclusions may remain inviolate. And therefore it was a good answer that was made by one who when they showed him hanging in a temple a picture of those who had paid their vows as having escaped shipwreck, and would have him say whether he did not now acknowledge the power of the gods,—"Aye," asked he again, "but where are they painted that were drowned after their vows?" And such is the way of all superstition, whether in astrology, dreams, omens, divine judgments, or the like; wherein men, having a delight in such vanities, mark the events where they are fulfilled, but where they fail, though this happen much oftener, neglect and pass them by. But with far more subtlety does this mischief insinuate itself into philosophy and the sciences; in which the first conclusion colours and brings into conformity with itself all that come after, though far sounder and better. Besides, independently of that delight and vanity which I have described it is the peculiar and perpetual error of the human intellect to be more moved and excited by affirmatives than by negatives; whereas it ought properly to hold itself indifferently disposed towards both alike. Indeed in the establishment of any true axiom, the negative instance is the more forcible of the two.

xlvii

The human understanding is moved by those things most which strike and enter the mind simultaneously and suddenly, and so fill the imagination; and then it feigns and supposes all other things to be somehow, though it cannot see how, similar to those few things by which it is surrounded. But for that going to and fro to remote and heterogeneous instances, by which axioms are tried as in the fire, the intellect is altogether slow and unfit, unless it be forced thereto by severe laws and overruling authority.

xlviii

The human understanding is unquiet; it cannot stop or rest, and still presses onward, but in vain. Therefore it is that we cannot conceive of any end or limit to the world, but always as of necessity it occurs to us that there is something beyond. Neither again can it be conceived how eternity has flowed down to the present day: for that distinction which is commonly received of infinity in time past and in time to come can by no means hold; for it would thence follow that one infinity is greater than another, and that infinity is wasting away and tending to become finite. The like subtlety arises touching the infinite divisibility of lines, from the same inability of thought to stop. But this inability interferes more mischievously in the discovery of causes: for although the most general principles in nature ought to be held merely positive, as they are discovered, and cannot with truth be referred to a cause; nevertheless the human understanding being unable to rest still seeks something prior in the order of nature. And then it is that in struggling towards that which is further off it falls back upon that which is more nigh at hand; namely, on final causes (or aims): which have relation clearly to the nature of man rather than to the nature of the universe; and from this source have strangely defiled philosophy. But he is no less an unskilled and shallow philosopher who seeks causes of that which is most general, than he who in things subordinate and subaltern omits to do so.

xlix

The human understanding is no dry light, but receives an infusion from the will and affections (or emotions); whence proceed sciences which may be called "sciences as one would." For what a man had rather were true he more readily believes. Therefore he rejects difficult things from impatience of research; sober things, because they narrow hope; the deeper things of nature, from superstition; the light of experience, from arrogance and pride, lest his mind should seem to be occupied with things mean and transitory; things not commonly believed, out of deference to the opinion of the vulgar. Numberless in short are the ways, and sometimes imperceptible, in which the affections colour and infect the understanding.

l

But by far the greatest hindrance and aberration of the human understanding proceeds from the dullness, incompetency, and deceptions of the senses; in that things which strike the sense outweigh things which do not immediately strike it, though they be more important. Hence it is that speculation commonly ceases where sight ceases; insomuch that of things invisible there is little or no observation. Hence all the working of the spirits inclosed in tangible bodies lies hid and unobserved of men. So also all the more subtle changes of form in the parts of coarser substances (which they commonly call alteration, though it is in truth local motion through exceedingly small spaces) is in like manner unobserved. And yet unless these two things just mentioned be searched out and brought to light, nothing great can be achieved in nature, as far as the production of works is concerned. So again the essential nature of our common air, and of all bodies less dense than air (which are very many), is almost unknown. For the sense by itself is a thing infirm and erring; neither can instruments for enlarging or sharpening the senses do much; but all the truer kind of interpretation of nature is effected by instances and experiments fit and opposite; wherein the sense decides touching the experiment only, and the experiment touching the point in nature and the thing itself.

li

The human understanding is of its own nature prone to abstractions and gives a substance and reality to things which are fleeting. But to resolve nature into abstractions is less to our purpose than to dissect her into parts; as did the school of Democritus, which went further into nature than the rest. Matter rather than forms should be the object of our attention, its configurations and changes of configuration, and simple action, and law of action or motion; for forms are figments of the human mind, unless you will call those laws of action forms.

lii

Such then are the idols which I call *Idols of the Tribe;* and which take their rise either from the homogeneity of the substance of the human spirit, or from its preoccupation, or from its narrowness, or from its restless motion, or from an infusion of the affections, or from the incompetency of the senses, or from the mode of impression.

liii

The *Idols of the Cave* take their rise in the peculiar constitution, mental or bodily, of each individual; and also in education, habit, and accident. Of this kind there is a great number and variety; but I will instance those the pointing out of which contains the most important caution, and which have most effect in disturbing the clearness of the understanding.

liv

Men become attached to certain particular sciences and speculations, either because they fancy themselves the authors and inventors thereof, or because they have bestowed the greatest pains upon them and become most habituated to them. But men of this kind, if they betake themselves to philosophy and contemplations of a general character, distort and colour them in obedience to their former fancies; a thing especially to be noticed in Aristotle, who made his natural philosophy a mere bond-servant to his logic, thereby rendering it contentious and well nigh useless. The race of chemists again out of a few experiments of the furnace have built up a fantastic philosophy, framed with reference to a few things; and Gilbert also, after he had employed himself most laboriously in the study and observation of the loadstone, proceeded at once to construct an entire system in accordance with his favourite subject.

lv

There is one principal and as it were radical distinction between different minds, in respect of philosophy and the sciences; which is this: that some minds are stronger and apter to mark the differences of things, others to mark their resemblances. The steady and acute mind can fix its contemplations and dwell and fasten on the subtlest distinctions; the lofty and discursive mind recognizes and puts together the finest and most general resemblances. Both kinds however, easily err in excess, by catching the one at gradations the other at shadows.

lvi

There are found some minds given to an extreme admiration of antiquity, others to an extreme love and appetite for novelty; but few so duly tempered that they can hold the mean, neither carping at what has been well laid down by the ancients, nor despising what is well introduced by the moderns. This however turns to the great injury of the sciences and philosophy: since these affectations of antiquity and novelty are the humours of partisans rather than judgments; and truth is to be sought for not in the felicity of any age, which is an unstable thing, but in the light of nature and experience, which is eternal. These factions therefore must be abjured, and care must be taken that the intellect be not hurried by them into assent.

lvii

Contemplations of nature and of bodies in their simple form break up and distract the understanding, while contemplations of nature and bodies in their composition and configuration overpower and dissolve the understanding: a distinction well seen in the school of Leucippus and Democritus as compared with the other philosophies. For that school is so busied with the particles that it hardly attends to the structure; while the others are so lost in admiration of the structure that they do not penetrate to the simplicity of nature. These kinds of contemplation should therefore be alternated and taken by turns; that so the understanding may be rendered at once penetrating and comprehensive, and the inconveniences above mentioned, with the idols which proceed from them, may be avoided.

lviii

Let such then be our provision and contemplative prudence for keeping off and dislodging the Idols of the Cave, which grow for the most part either out of the predominance of a favourite subject, or out of an excessive tendency to compare or to distinguish, or out of partiality for particular ages, or out of the largeness or minuteness of the objects contemplated. And generally let every student of nature take this as a rule,—that whatever his mind seizes and dwells upon with peculiar satisfaction is to be held in suspicion, and that so much the more care is to be taken in dealing with such questions to keep the understanding even and clear.

lix

But the *Idols of the Market-place* are the most troublesome of all: idols which have crept into the understanding through the alliances of words and names. For men believe that their reason governs words; but it is also true that words react on the understanding; and this it is that has rendered philosophy and the sciences sophistical and inactive. Now words, being commonly framed and applied according to the capacity of the vulgar, follow those lines of division which are most obvious to the vulgar understanding. And whenever an understanding of greater acuteness or a more diligent observation would alter those lines to suit the true divisions of nature, words stand in the way and resist the change. Whence it comes to pass that the high and formal discussions of learned men end oftentimes in disputes about words and names; with which (according to the use and wisdom of the mathematicians) it would be more prudent to begin, and so by means of definitions reduce them to order. Yet even definitions cannot cure this evil in dealing with natural and material things; since the definitions themselves consist of words, and those words beget others: so that it is necessary to recur to individual instances, and those in due series and order. . . .

lx

The Idols imposed by words on the understanding are of two kinds. They are either names of things which do not exist (for as there are things left unnamed through lack of observation, so likewise are there names which result from fantastic suppositions and to which nothing in reality corresponds), or they are names of things which exist, but yet confused and ill-defined, and hastily and irregularly derived from realities. Of the former kind are Fortune, the Prime Mover, Planetary Orbits, Element of Fire, and like fictions which owe their origin to false and idle theories. And this class of idols is more easily expelled, because to get rid of them it is only necessary that all theories should be steadily rejected and dismissed as obsolete.

But the other class, which springs out of a faulty and unskillful abstraction, is intricate and deeply rooted. Let us take for example such a word as *humid,* and see how far the several things which the word is used to signify agree with each other; and we shall find the word *humid* to be nothing else than a mark loosely and confusedly applied to denote a variety of actions which will not bear to be reduced to any constant meaning. For it both signifies that which easily spreads itself round any other body; and that which in itself is indeterminate and cannot solidise; and that which readily yields in every direction; and that which easily divides and scatters itself; and that which easily unites and collects itself; and that which readily flows and is put in motion; and that which readily clings to another body and wets it; and that which is easily reduced to a liquid, or being solid easily melts. Accordingly when you come to apply the word,—if you take it in one sense, flame is humid; if in another, air is not humid; if in another, fine dust is humid; if in another, glass is humid. So that it is easy to see that the notion is taken by abstraction only from water and common and ordinary liquids, without any due verification.

There are however in words certain degrees of distortion and error. One of the least faulty kinds is that of names of substances, especially of lowest species and well-deduced (for the notion of *chalk* and of *mud* is good, of *earth* bad); a more faulty kind is that of actions, as *to generate, to corrupt, to alter;* the most faulty is of qualities (except such as are the immediate objects of the sense) as *heavy, light, rare, dense,* and the like. Yet in all these cases some notions are of necessity a little better than others, in proportion to the greater variety of subjects that fall within the range of the human sense.

lxi

But the *Idols of the Theatre* are not innate, nor do they steal into the understanding secretly, but are plainly impressed and received into the mind from the play-books of philosophical systems and the perverted rules of demonstration. To attempt refutations in this case would be merely inconsistent with what I have already said: for since we agree neither upon principles nor upon demonstrations there is no place for argument. And this is so far well, inasmuch as it leaves the honour of the ancients untouched. For they are no wise disparaged —the question between them and me being only as to the way. For as the saying is, the lame man who keeps the right road outstrips the runner who takes a wrong one. Nay it is obvious that when a man runs the wrong way, the more active and swift he is the further he will go astray.

But the course I propose for the discovery of sciences is such as leaves but little to the acuteness and strength of wits, but places all wits and understandings nearly on a level. For as in the drawing of a straight line or a perfect circle, much depends on the steadiness and practice of the hand, if it be done by aim of hand only, but if with the aid of rule or compass, little or nothing; so is it exactly with my plan. But though particular confutations would be of no avail, yet touching the sects and general divisions of such systems I must say something; something also touching the external signs which show that they are unsound; and finally something touching the causes of such great infelicity and of such lasting and general agreement in error; that so the access to truth may be made less difficult, and the human understanding may the more willingly submit to its purgation and dismiss its idols.

lxii

Idols of the Theatre, or of Systems, are many, and there can be and perhaps will be yet many more. For were it not that now for many ages men's minds have been busied with religion and theology; and were it not that civil governments, especially monarchies, have been averse to such novelties, even in matters speculative; so that men labour therein to the peril and harming of their fortunes,—not only unrewarded, but exposed also to contempt and envy: doubtless there would have arisen many other philosophical sects like to those which in great variety flourished once among the Greeks. For as on the phenomena of the heavens many hypotheses may be constructed, so likewise (and more also) many various dogmas may be set up and established on the phenomena of philosophy. And in the plays of this philosophical theatre you may observe the same thing which is found in the theatre of the poets, that stories invented for the stage are more compact and elegant, and more as one would wish them to be, than true stories out of history.

In general however there is taken for the material of philosophy either a great deal out of a few things, or a very little out of many things; so that on both sides philosophy is based on too narrow a foundation of experiment and natural history, and decides on the authority of too few cases. For the Rational School of philosophers snatches from experience a variety of common instances, neither duly ascertained nor diligently examined and weighed, and leaves all the rest to meditation and agitation of wit.

There is also another class of philosophers, who having bestowed much diligent and careful labour on a few experiments, have thence made bold to educe and construct system; wresting all other facts in a strange fashion to conformity therewith.

And there is yet a third class, consisting of those who out of faith and veneration mix their philosophy with theology and traditions; among whom the vanity of some has gone so far aside as to seek the origin of sciences among spirits and genii. So that this parent stock of errors—this false philosophy—is of three kinds; the Sophistical, the Empirical, and the Superstitious.

2

SCIENCE HAS A HISTORY

The literature on the history of science is voluminous; it is also expanding rapidly, for in relatively recent years the history of science has been recognized as a specialized field of scholarship, and a number of scientist-historians, here and abroad, are devoting their lives to its systematic study. One might make a case that no man can properly be regarded as educated until he knows at least the general historical outlines of the institution that is modern science—an institution now of overwhelming significance to all facets of human life.

In this limited space, it will be possible only to indicate that science has a history, and that there may be many ways to analyze that history. When a subtle and informed mind investigates that history, some surprising things come to light. Who would have thought, for example, that science as we know it may owe its existence to the unquestioning and prevailing medieval belief in the rationality of God?

The following excerpts from the writing of Alfred North Whitehead point out among other things that modern science came into existence when there arose (a) a concern for precise and stubborn fact to accompany (b) the already existing and more philosophically respectable search for all-encompassing principles. Philosophers of science tell us that these two trends, presented here as historical developments, remain as the two necessary components of modern science. Some scientists espouse with great fervor the world of stubborn fact, and assert that knowledge advances through the gradual and inexorable accumulation of hard factual bits. Others are temperamentally more inclined to generalization, broad interpretation, and theory, and when pressed, may denigrate the significance of mere fact. Whitehead and other historians and philosophers of science suggest that science not only was born of an interaction of these two trends but also that science lives and advances through the continuation of that interaction.

THE ORIGINS OF MODERN SCIENCE*

Alfred North Whitehead

When he [William James] was finishing his great treatise on the *Principles of Psychology,* he wrote to his brother Henry James, "I have to forge every sentence in the teeth of irreducible and stubborn facts."

This new tinge to modern minds is a vehement and passionate interest in the relation of general principles to irreducible and stubborn facts. All the world over and at all times there have been practical men, absorbed in "irreducible and stubborn facts": all the world over and at all times there have been men of philosophic temperament who have been absorbed in the weaving of general principles. It is this union of passionate interest in the detailed facts with equal devotion to abstract generalisation which forms the novelty in our present society. Previously it had appeared sporadically and as if by chance. This balance of mind has now become part of the tradition which infects cultivated thought. It is the salt which keeps life sweet. The main business of universities is to transmit this tradition as a widespread inheritance from generation to generation. . . .

Another contrast which singles out science from among the European movements of the sixteenth and seventeenth centuries is its universality. Modern science was born in Europe, but its home is the whole world. In the last two centuries there has been a long and confused impact of western modes upon the civilisation of Asia. The wise men of the East have been puzzling, and are puzzling, as to what may be the regulative secret of life which can be passed from West to East without the wanton destruction of their own inheritance which they so rightly prize. More and more it is becoming evident that what the West can most readily give to the East is its science and its scientific outlook. This is transferable from country to country, and from race to race, wherever there is a rational society. . . .

Obviously, the main recurrences of life are too insistent to escape the notice of the least rational of humans; and even before the dawn

* Excerpts reprinted with permission of The Macmillan Company and of Cambridge University Press from *Science and the Modern World* by Alfred North Whitehead.

of rationality, they have impressed themselves upon the instincts of animals. It is unnecessary to labour the point, that in broad outline certain general states of nature recur, and that our very natures have adapted themselves to such repetitions.

But there is a complementary fact which is equally true and equally obvious:—nothing ever really recurs in exact detail. No two days are identical, no two winters. What has gone, has gone forever. Accordingly the practical philosophy of mankind has been to expect the broad recurrences, and to accept the details as emanating from the inscrutable womb of things beyond the ken of rationality. Men expected the sun to rise, but the wind bloweth where it listeth.

Certainly from the classical Greek civilisation onwards there have been men, and indeed groups of men, who have placed themselves beyond this acceptance of an ultimate irrationality. Such men have endeavoured to explain all phenomena as the outcome of an order of things which extends to every detail. Geniuses such as Aristotle, or Archimedes, or Roger Bacon, must have been endowed with the full scientific mentality, which instinctively holds that all things great and small are conceivable as exemplifications of general principles which reign throughout the natural order.

But until the close of the Middle Ages the general educated public did not feel that intimate conviction, and that detailed interest, in such an idea, so as to lead to an unceasing supply of men, with ability and opportunity adequate to maintain a coordinated search for the discovery of these hypothetical principles. Either people were doubtful about the existence of such principles, or were doubtful about any success in finding them, or took no interest in thinking about them, or were oblivious to their practical importance when found. For whatever reason, search was languid, if we have regard to the opportunities of a high civilisation and the length of time concerned. Why did the pace suddenly quicken in the sixteenth and seventeenth centuries? At the close of the Middle Ages a new mentality discloses itself. Invention stimulated thought, thought quickened physical speculation, Greek manuscripts disclosed what the ancients had discovered. Finally, although in the year 1500 Europe knew less than Archimedes who died in the year 212 B.C., yet in the year 1700, Newton's *Principia* had been written and the world was well started on the modern epoch. . . .

Galileo keeps harping on how things happen, whereas his adversaries had a complete theory as to why things happen. Unfortunately the two theories did not bring out the same results. Galileo insists upon "irreducible and stubborn facts," and Simplicius, his opponent, brings forward reasons, completely satisfactory, at least to himself. . . .

But for science something more is wanted than a general sense of the order in things. It needs but a sentence to point out how the habit of definite exact thought was implanted in the European mind by the long dominance of scholastic logic and scholastic divinity. The habit remained after the philosophy had been repudiated, the priceless habit of looking for an exact point and of sticking to it when found. Galileo owes more to Aristotle than appears on the surface of his *Dialogues:* he owes to him his clear head and his analytic mind. . . .

I do not think, however, that I have even yet brought out the greatest contribution of medievalism to the formation of the scientific movement. I mean the inexpugnable belief that every detailed occurrence can be correlated with its antecedents in a perfectly definite manner, exemplifying general principles. Without this belief the incredible labours of scientists would be without hope. It is this instinctive conviction, vividly poised before the imagination, which is the motive power of research: —that there is a secret, a secret which can be unveiled. How has this conviction been so vividly implanted on the European mind?

When we compare this tone of thought in Europe with the attitude of other civilisations when left to themselves, there seems but one source for its origin. It must come from the medieval insistence on the rationality of God, conceived as with the personal energy of Jehovah and with the rationality of a Greek philosopher. Every detail was supervised and ordered: the search into nature could only result in the vindication of the faith in rationality. Remember that I am not talking of the explicit beliefs of a few individuals. What I mean is the impress on the European mind arising from the unquestioned faith of centuries. By this I mean the instinctive tone of thought and not a mere creed of words.

In Asia, the conceptions of God were of a being who was either too arbitrary or too impersonal for such ideas to have much effect on instinctive habits of mind. Any definite occurrence might be due to the fiat of an irrational despot, or might issue from some impersonal, inscrutable origin of things. There was not the same confidence as in the intelligible rationality of a personal being. I am not arguing that the European trust in the scrutability of nature was logically justified even by its own theology. My only point is to understand how it arose. My explanation is that the faith in the possibility of science, generated antecedently to the development of modern scientific theory, is an unconscious derivative from medieval theology. . . .

The truth is that science started its modern career by taking over ideas derived from the weakest side of the philosophies of Aristotle's successors. In some respects it was a happy choice. It enabled the knowledge of the seventeenth century to be formularized so far as physics and chemistry were concerned, with a completeness which has lasted to the present time. But the progress of biology and psychology has probably been checked by the uncritical assumption of half-truths. If science is not to degenerate into a medley of *ad hoc* hypotheses, it must become philosophical and must enter upon a thorough criticism of its own foundations. . . .

3

SCIENTIFIC AND OTHER APPROACHES TO KNOWLEDGE

The attitudes, approaches, and methods of the scientist set him apart from others who seek understanding, and all help to make the products of his creative efforts appreciably different from the products of the rational philosopher, the theologian, or the artist. For, although it would be difficult to defend the position that either the scientific approach or its products possess an everlasting and demonstrable superiority to other approaches and other products, there clearly is a distinctively scientific approach and a distinctively scientific product. The following excerpt from the writings of James B. Conant helps indicate the special attributes of the scientific enterprise and the uniqueness of the products of scientific endeavor. The selection from the writings of Hans Reichenbach, eminent philosopher of science, will go further into both the distinctions and the relationships between the empirical and the rationalistic approaches to knowledge. Then we return again to Alfred North Whitehead for a view of the contrasts and relationships between science and religion.

ACCUMULATIVE KNOWLEDGE, PHILOSOPHY, AND POETRY*

James B. Conant

A certain degree of unity can be achieved in the learned world by emphasizing the fact that knowledge has indeed advanced in many

* Excerpted from James B. Conant, *On Understanding Science*. New Haven: Yale University Press, 1947. Pp. 20–21, 24–27. By permission.

areas in the last three hundred years. From this point of view alone there would be great advantages in having the case histories chosen from as many fields as possible. I have suggested on another occasion that one may group together under the heading "accumulative knowledge" subjects as diverse as mathematics, physics, chemistry, biology, anthropology, philology, and archaeology. One can state with assurance that great advances have been made in these subjects in the last three centuries. A similar statement cannot be made about philosophy, poetry, and the fine arts. If you are inclined to doubt this and raise the question of how progress even in academic matters can be defined, I would respond by asking you to perform an imaginary operation. Bring back to life the great figures of the past who were identified with the subjects in question. Ask them to view the present scene and answer whether or not in their opinion there has been an advance. No one can doubt how Galileo, Newton, Harvey, or the pioneers in anthropology and archaeology would respond. It is far otherwise with Michelangelo, Rembrandt, Dante, Milton, or Keats. It would be otherwise with Thomas Aquinas, Spinoza, Locke, or Kant. We might argue all day whether or not the particular artist or poet or philosopher would feel the present state of art or poetry or philosophy to be an advance or a retrogression from the days when he himself was a creative spirit. There would be no unanimity among us; and more significant still, no agreement between the majority view which might prevail and that which would have prevailed fifty years ago. . . .

As a first approximation, we may say that science emerges from the other progressive activities of man to the extent that new concepts arise from experiments and observations, and the new concepts in turn lead to further experiments and observations. The case histories drawn from the last three hundred years show examples of fruitful and fruitless concepts. The texture of modern science is the result of the interweaving of the fruitful concepts. The test of a new idea is therefore not only its success in correlating the then-known facts but much more its success or failure in stimulating further experimentation or observation which in turn is fruitful. This dynamic quality of science viewed not as a practical undertaking but as development of conceptual schemes seems to me to be close to the heart of the best definition. It is this quality which can be demonstrated only by the historical approach, or else learned by direct professional experience.

To illustrate what I have in mind let us imagine a period in the future when all interest in scientific investigation had ceased but the relatively simple conceptual schemes about matter and energy, the solar system and the basic facts of chemistry of the late nineteenth century were accepted and widely taught. Would the people of that day "understand" science as the late Victorians did? Not to my mind. There would be little difference in their intellectual outlook from that of a people who accept their cosmology as part of a revealed religion. If this be so, the characteristic of the scientific age in which we live lies not in the relative adequacies of our conceptual schemes as to the universe but in the dynamic character of these concepts as interpreted by both professional scientists and laymen. Almost by definition, I would say, science moves ahead.

THE EMPIRICIST APPROACH: SUCCESS AND FAILURE*

Hans Reichenbach

The philosophers thus far referred to [Hegel, Kant, Spinoza, *et al.*] are selected from a certain point of view; they exhibit a specific type of philosophy and must not be considered as representing philosophy as a whole. Their philosophy is characterized by the conception that there exists a special domain of knowledge, philosophical knowledge, which the human mind acquires through the use of a particular capacity, called reason, or intuition, or vision of ideas. The systems of these philosophers are the alleged products of this capacity; they are believed to supply a sort of knowledge which the scientist cannot attain, a superscientific knowledge inaccessible to the methods of sense observation and generalization by which the sciences are constructed. This kind of philosophy was here denoted by the name of *rationalism*. For the rationalist, apart from a few exceptions like Hegel, mathematics represents the ideal form of knowledge; it supplies the pattern after which philosophical knowledge is modeled.

From the time of the Greeks, however, there has existed a second type of philosophy which is essentially different from the first. The philosophers of the second type regard empirical science, and not mathematics, as the ideal form of knowledge; they insist that sense

* Excerpted from Hans Reichenbach, *The Rise of Scientific Philosophy*. Berkeley: University of California Press, 1956. By permission.

observation is the primary source and the ultimate judge of knowledge, and that it is self-deception to believe the human mind to have a direct access to any kind of truth other than that of empty logical relations. This type of philosophy is called *empiricism.*

The empiricist method differs radically from that of rationalism. The empiricist philosopher does not claim to discover a new kind of knowledge inaccessible to the scientist; he merely studies and analyzes observational knowledge, be it scientific or commonplace, and tries to understand its meaning and its implications. He does not mind if the theory of knowledge thus constructed is called philosophical knowledge; but he regards it as constructed by the same methods as employed by the scientist and refuses to interpret it as the product of a specific philosophical capacity.

Not always has the empiricist thesis been so clearly stated as we can state it now; the elaboration of the thesis of empiricism is in itself the product of a long historical development. The older empiricists did not possess the clear conception of empirical science which we have today, and were frequently influenced by rationalist systems. Furthermore, their philosophy often included parts which we regard today as belonging in empirical science, such as theories of the origin of the universe or of the nature of matter. Of this kind were the systems of the Greek empiricists, whom we find both in the pre-Socratic and later periods of Greek philosophy. The most prominent among them is Democritus, a contemporary of Socrates, who is regarded as the first to conceive of the idea that nature consists of atoms and hence has a place in the history of science as well as in the history of philosophy. His cosmogony is outstanding because it assumes an evolution through the combination of atoms into complicated structures. Originally, there were only individual atoms traveling in all directions through space; through chance collisions, vortices developed which eventually led to the formation of bodies of all kinds and shapes. These ideas were taken up, some one hundred years later, by Epicurus, whose system was transmitted, in Roman times, to later generations, through Lucretius' famous poem *De Rerum Natura.* Epicurus gave a somewhat different version of the movement of the atoms in assuming that the atoms were originally all falling down along parallel lines for an infinite time, until by chance some atoms deviated from their paths and collided with others. This chance event started evolution.

Among later Greek philosophers, the skeptics may be regarded as representatives of empiricism. If they questioned the possibility of knowledge, it was because the Greeks identified knowledge with absolutely certain knowledge. Carneades (second century B.C.) recognized that deduction cannot supply such knowledge because it merely derives conclusions from given premises and cannot establish the truth of the axioms. He saw, moreover, that for the purpose of an orientation in everyday life absolute knowledge is unnecessary and that well-established opinion suffices as a basis for actions. From this point of view he developed a theory of probability which distinguished three kinds of probability, or degrees of certainty. With his defense of opinion and probability Carneades laid the foundations of the empiricist position in an intellectual environment where mathematical certainty was regarded the only permissible form of knowledge. Developed in constant clash with the prevalent rationalist doctrines, the conceptions of these early empiricists were predominantly skeptical; they exhibit the healthy but albeit negative trait of an attack against rationalism and do not go far in the construction of a positive empiricist philosophy.

The school of skeptics was continued through the centuries; some three hundred years after Carneades, Sextus Empiricus (about 150 A.D.) wrote a synopsis of the skeptical doctrines, which informs us about his early predecessors and leaves no doubt that the author does not want to question the possibility of purposive action based on information derived from sense perception. He is also a leading representative of the school of empirical physicians, who attempted to purify the science of medicine from speculative additions. The Arabic philosophers include empiricists such as Alhazen, famous for his work in physiological optics. During the Middle Ages, philosophy was carried on by clerics only, and scholastic philosophy thus has not much room for empiricism. Men like Roger Bacon, Peter Aureoli, and William of Occam, who courageously attempted to defend the empiricist position, are too deeply imbued with theological modes of thought to be comparable with the empiricists of an earlier or a later time. This remark is not intended to belittle the historical significance of these men; in fact, if merit is measured by the deviation of a man's views from environmental opinions, their stand for empiricism deserves the admiration of all those who have been empiricists in more empirically minded periods.

The close connection between rationalism and theology is understandable. Since religious doctrines are not based on sense perception, they demand an extrasensory source of knowledge. The philosopher who pretends to have found a knowledge of this type is the natural ally of the theologian. The systems of the great Greek rationalists Plato and Aristotle were utilized by Christian theologians for the construction of a philosophy of Christianity; Plato became the philosopher of more mystically minded groups, Aristotle that of scholasticism. The relation to theology has at all times made the rationalist feel himself superior to the empiricist in a moral sense. The antagonism between the two groups, though felt on one side as strongly as on the other, is not of a symmetrical form; whereas the rationalist regards the empiricist as morally inferior, the empiricist regards the rationalist as devoid of common sense.

It was with the rise of modern science, about the year 1600, that empiricism began to assume the form of a positive and well-founded philosophical theory which could enter into successful competition with rationalism. The modern period has given us the great empiricist systems of Francis Bacon (1561–1626), John Locke (1632–1704), and David Hume (1711–1776). The positions of these British empiricists must now be compared with rationalism.

The thesis of empiricism found its clear elaboration in the philosophies of these men. The conception that perception is the source and the ultimate test of knowledge is the eventual result of their work. The mind, says Locke, begins as a blank page; it is experience that writes on this paper. Nothing is in the mind that was not previously in the senses. There are, however, two kinds of sense perception: perception of external and of internal objects. The latter kind of object is given by psychological occurrences, like thinking, believing, the feeling of pain, or the sensation of color, which we observe through an internal sense. Hume divides the contents of the mind into impressions and ideas; the impressions are supplied by the senses, including the internal sense, and the ideas are recollections of previous impressions. Only in their combination can ideas differ from observed phenomena. For instance, the observed impressions of gold and of a mountain can be put together to form the unobserved, but imaginable, combination of a golden mountain. In contrast to rationalism, empiricism thus reduces the mind to the subordinate role of establishing an order between impressions and ideas; the ordered system is what we call knowledge.

The function of the mind in the construction of knowledge may be illustrated by some examples which could have been used by Bacon, Locke, or Hume. Among the various experiences of a day, the mind picks out the brightness of fire as seen by the eyes and associates it with the feeling of heat perceived when we are close to a fire, thus arriving at the physical law that fire is hot. Similarly, the mind discovers the laws of the motions of the stars by comparing the various pictures we observe in looking at the night sky at different hours and days; in connecting the various positions of a star by imaginary lines, the mind plots the star's path, which in itself is not an object of observation.

When I say that mind is allotted a subordinate role in this conception of knowledge, I mean to say that mind is not regarded as the judge of truth. To the mind, a circle may appear as the most worthy form for the motion of a star; but whether this motion is actually circular is judged by perception. Reason may induce me to say that matter consists of small particles, because otherwise I do not see how matter can be compressible; but whether atomism is true must be judged by perceptions. In this instance perception cannot directly answer the question, because atoms are too small to be observable; but it answers the question indirectly by supplying us with a set of observable facts that make the atomic interpretation unavoidable. The latter instance, however, makes it obvious that the function of mind in the construction of knowledge cannot be called subordinate in another sense: reason is an indispensable instrument for the organization of knowledge, without which facts of a more abstract kind could not be known. The senses do not show me that the planets move in ellipses around the sun, or that matter consists of atoms; it is sense observation in combination with reasoning that leads to such abstract truths.

Bacon saw very clearly the indispensability of reason for an empiricist conception of knowledge. In a discussion of philosophical systems he compares the rationalists with spiders that make cobwebs out of their own substance, the older empiricists with ants that collect material without being able to find an order in it; the new empiricists, he claims, are like the bees that gather material and digest it, adding to it from their own substance and thus creating a product of a higher quality. That is a great program stated in a witty form. Let us see how far the empiricism of the seventeenth and eighteenth century has lived up to it.

What is the addition that reason makes to observational knowledge? We said it is the introduction of abstract relations of order. However, abstract relations in themselves would not be so interesting if they did not include statements of new concreta. If the abstract relations are general truths, they hold not only for the observations made, but also for observations not yet made; they include not only an account of past experiences, but also predictions of future experiences. That is the addition which reason makes to knowledge. Observation informs us about the past and the present; reason foretells the future.

Let me illustrate the predictive nature of abstract laws by some examples. The law that fire is hot goes beyond the experiences on which this law was established and which belong to the past; it predicts that whenever we shall see a fire it will be hot. The laws of the motion of the stars permit us to predict the future positions of the stars and include predictions of observations like eclipses of the sun and the moon. The atomic theory of matter has led to chemical predictions, verified in the construction of new chemical substances; in fact, all industrial applications of science are based on the predictive nature of scientific laws, since they employ scientific laws as blue-prints for the construction of devices that function according to a preconceived plan. Bacon had a clear insight into the predictive nature of knowledge when he coined his famous maxim: knowledge is power.

How can reason predict the future? Bacon saw that reason alone does not have any predictive capacity; it gains it only in combination with observation. The predictive methods of reason are contained in the logical operations by means of which we construct an order into the observational material and derive conclusions. We arrive at predictions through the instrument of the logical derivation. Bacon recognized, furthermore, that if logical derivation is to serve predictive purposes, it cannot be restricted to *deductive logic;* it must include methods of an *inductive logic.*

This distinction, on which the development of modern empiricism hinges, may be made clearer by a consideration of the syllogism. Consider the classic example: "All men are mortal, Socrates is a man, therefore Socrates is mortal." As explained above, the conclusion is analytically implied by the premises and does not add anything to them. It merely makes some part of their content explicit. Such emptiness is the very essence of deductive inference and represents the price which we pay for the necessary truth of the conclusion. Consider, in contrast, the inference "all crows so far observed were black, therefore all crows in the world are black." The conclusion is not contained in the premise; it refers to crows not yet observed and extends to them a property of the observed crows. Consequently, the truth of the conclusion cannot be guaranteed; it is possible that some day we might discover in a remote wilderness a bird that possesses all properties of a crow except for the black color. In spite of this possibility we are willing to make this kind of inference, especially when more important things than crows are concerned. We need it if we want to establish a general truth, which includes a reference to unobserved things, and because we need it, we are willing to take the risk of an error.

RELIGION AND SCIENCE*

Alfred North Whitehead

The difficulty in approaching the question of the relations between Religion and Science is, that its elucidation requires that we have in our minds some clear idea of what we mean by either of the terms, "religion" and "science." Also I wish to speak in the most general way possible, and to keep in the background any comparison of particular creeds, scientific or religious. We have got to understand the type of connection which exists between the two spheres, and then to draw some definite conclusions respecting the existing situation which at present confronts the world.

The *conflict* between religion and science is what naturally occurs to our minds when we think of this subject. It seems as though, during the last half-century, the results of science and the beliefs of religion had come into a position of frank disagreement, from which there can be no escape, except by abandoning either the clear teaching of science, or the clear teaching of religion. This conclusion has been urged by controversialists on either side. Not by all controversialists, of course, but by those trenchant intellects which every controversy calls out into the open.

The distress of sensitive minds, and the zeal for truth, and the sense of the importance of the issues, must command our sincerest sympathy. When we consider what religion is for mankind, and what science is, it is no exaggeration to say that the future course of history depends upon the decision of this generation as to the relations between them. We have here the two strongest general forces (apart

* Excerpts reprinted with permission of The Macmillan Company and of Cambridge University Press from *Science and the Modern World* by Alfred North Whitehead.

from the mere impulse of the various senses) which influence men, and they seem to be set one against the other—the force of our religious intuitions, and the force of our impulse to accurate observation and logical deduction.

A great English statesman once advised his countrymen to use large-scale maps, as a preservative against alarms, panics, and general misunderstanding of the true relations between nations. In the same way in dealing with the clash between permanent elements of human nature, it is well to map our history on a large scale, and to disengage ourselves from our immediate absorption in the present conflicts. When we do this, we immediately discover two great facts. In the first place, there has always been a conflict between religion and science; and in the second place, both religion and science have always been in a state of continual development. In the early days of Christianity, there was a general belief among Christians that the world was coming to an end in the lifetime of people then living. We can make only indirect inferences as to how far this belief was authoritatively proclaimed; but it is certain that it was widely held, and that it formed an impressive part of the popular religious doctrine. The belief proved itself to be mistaken, and the Christian doctrine adjusted itself to the change. Again in the early Church individual theologians very confidently deduced from the Bible opinions concerning the nature of the physical universe. In the year A.D. 535, a monk named Cosmas wrote a book which he entitled, *Christian Topography*. He was a travelled man who had visited India and Ethiopia; and finally he lived in a monastery at Alexandria, which was then a great centre of culture. In this book, basing himself upon the direct meaning of Biblical texts as construed by him in a literal fashion, he denied the existence of the antipodes, and asserted that the world is a flat parallelogram whose length is double its breadth.

In the seventeenth century the doctrine of the motion of the earth was condemned by a Catholic tribunal. A hundred years ago the extension of time demanded by geological science distressed religious people, Protestant and Catholic. And today the doctrine of evolution is an equal stumbling-block. These are only a few instances illustrating a general fact. . . .

Science is even more changeable than theology. No man of science could subscribe without qualification to Galileo's beliefs, or to Newton's beliefs, or to all his own scientific beliefs of ten years ago.

In both regions of thought, additions, distinctions, and modifications have been introduced. So that now, even when the same assertion is made today as it was made a thousand, or fifteen hundred years ago, it is made subject to limitations or expansions of meaning, which were not contemplated at the earlier epoch. . . .

We would believe nothing in either sphere of thought which does not appear to us to be certified by solid reasons based upon the critical research either of ourselves or of competent authorities. But granting that we have honestly taken this precaution, a clash between the two on points of detail where they overlap should not lead us hastily to abandon doctrines for which we have solid evidence. It may be that we are more interested in one set of doctrines than in the other. But, if we have any sense of perspective and of the history of thought, we shall wait and refrain from mutual anathemas.

We should wait: but we should not wait passively, or in despair. The clash is a sign that there are wider truths and finer perspectives within which a reconciliation of a deeper religion and a more subtle science will be found. . . .

A clash of doctrines is not a disaster—it is an opportunity. . . .

Religion will not regain its old power until it can face change in the same spirit as does science. Its principles may be eternal, but the expression of those principles requires continual development. This evolution of religion is in the main a disengagement of its own proper ideas from the adventitious notions which have crept into it by reason of the expression of its own ideas in terms of the imaginative picture of the world entertained in previous ages. Such a release of religion from the bonds of imperfect science is all to the good. It stresses its own genuine message. The great point to be kept in mind is that normally an advance in science will show that statements of various religious beliefs require some sort of modification. It may be that they have to be expanded or explained, or indeed entirely restated. If the religion is a sound expression of truth, this modification will only exhibit more adequately the exact point which is of importance. This process is a gain. In so far, therefore, as any religion has any contact with physical facts, it is to be expected that the point of view of those facts must be continually modified as scientific knowledge advances. In this way, the exact relevance of these facts for religious thought will grow more and more clear. The progress of science must result in the unceasing codification of religious thought to the great advantage of religion. . . .

4

SCIENCE INVOLVES COMMUNICATION

Neither science nor any other form of organized human activity could exist were it not for symbols, and for the shared, patterned systems of symbols that constitute human languages. The following excerpts from S. I. Hayakawa may help to explain some of the scientist's concern with matters of semantics, definition, and logic. Perhaps Alfred North Whitehead, in this additional excerpt, can elucidate the often heard and incompletely understood reference to mathematics as the language of science.

LANGUAGE IN THOUGHT AND ACTION*

S. I. Hayakawa

Once upon a time (said the Professor), there were two small communities, spiritually as well as geographically situated at a considerable distance from each other. They had, however, these problems in common: Both were hard hit by a depression, so that in each of the towns there were about one hundred heads of families unemployed. There was, to be sure, enough food, enough clothing, enough materials for housing, but these families simply did not have money to procure these necessities.

The city fathers of A-town, the first community, were substantial businessmen, moderately well educated, good to their families, kind-hearted, and sound-thinking. The unemployed tried hard, as unemployed people usually do, to find jobs; but the situation did not improve. The city fathers, as well as the unemployed themselves, had been brought up to believe that there is always enough work for everyone, if you only look for it hard enough. Comforting themselves with this doctrine, the city fathers could have shrugged their shoulders and turned their backs on the problem, except for the fact that they were genuinely kindhearted men. They could not bear to see the unemployed men and their wives and children starving. In order to prevent starvation, they felt that they had to provide these people with some means of sustenance. Their principles told them, nevertheless, that if people were given something for nothing, it would demoralize their character. Naturally this made the city fathers even more unhappy, because they were faced with the horrible choice of (1) letting the unemployed starve, or (2) destroying their moral character.

The solution they finally hit upon, after much debate and soul-searching, was this. They decided to give the unemployed families relief of fifty dollars a month; but to insure against the pauperization of the recipients, they decided that this fifty dollars was to be accompanied by a moral lesson, to wit: the obtaining of the assistance would be made so difficult, humiliating, and disagreeable that there would be no temptation for anyone to go through the process unless it was absolutely necessary; the moral disapproval of the community would be turned upon the recipients of the money at all times in such a way that they would try hard to get off relief and regain their self-respect. Some even proposed that people on relief be denied the vote, so that the moral lesson would be more deeply impressed upon them. Others suggested that their names be published at regular intervals in the newspapers, so that there would be a strong incentive to get off relief. The city fathers had enough faith in the goodness of human nature to expect that the recipients would be grateful, since they were getting something for nothing, something which they hadn't worked for.

When the plan was put into operation, however, the recipients of the relief checks proved to be an ungrateful, ugly bunch. They seemed to resent the cross-examinations and inspections at the hands of the relief investigators, who, they said, took advantage of a man's misery to snoop into every detail of his private life. In spite of uplifting editorials in A-town *Tribune* telling them how grateful they ought to be, the recipients of the relief refused to learn any moral lessons, declaring that they were "just as good as anybody else." When, for example, they permitted themselves the rare luxury of a movie or an evening of bingo, their neighbors looked at them sourly as if to say, "I work hard and pay my taxes just in order to support loafers like you in idleness and pleasure." This attitude, which was fairly characteristic of those members of the community who still had jobs, further embittered the relief recipients, so that they showed even less gratitude as time went on and were constantly on the lookout for insults, real or imaginary, from people who might think that they weren't as good as anybody else. A number of them took to moping all day long, to thinking that their lives had been failures; one or two even committed suicide. Others found that it was hard to look their wives and kiddies in the face, because they had failed to provide. They all found it difficult to maintain their club and fraternal relationships, since they could not help feeling that their fellow citizens despised them for having sunk so low. Their wives, too, were unhappy for the same reasons and gave up their social activities. Children whose parents were on relief felt inferior to classmates whose parents were not public charges. Some of these children developed inferiority complexes which affected not only their grades at school, but their careers after graduation. Several other relief recipients, finally, felt they could stand their loss of self-respect no longer and decided, after many efforts to gain honest jobs, to earn money by their own efforts, even if they had to go in for robbery. They did so and were caught and sent to the state penitentiary.

The depression, therefore, hit A-town very hard. The relief policy had averted starvation, no doubt, but suicide, personal quarrels, unhappy homes, the weakening of social organizations, the maladjustment of children, and, finally, crime, had resulted. The town was divided in two, the "haves" and the "have-nots," so that there was class hatred. People shook their heads sadly and declared that it all went to prove over again what they had known from the beginning, that giving people something for nothing inevitably demoralizes their character. The citizens of A-town gloomily waited for prosperity to return, with less and less hope as time went on.

The story of the other community, B-ville, was entirely different. B-ville was a relatively isolated town, too far out of the way to be reached by Rotary Club speakers and university extension services. One of the aldermen, however, who was something of an economist, explained to his fellow aldermen that unemployment, like sickness, accident, fire, tornado, or death, hits unexpectedly in modern society, irrespective of the victim's merits or deserts. He went on to say that

B-ville's homes, parks, streets, industries, and everything else B-ville was proud of had been built in part by the work of these same people who were now unemployed. He then proposed to apply a principle of insurance: If the work these unemployed people had previously done for the community could be regarded as a form of premium paid to the community against a time of misfortune, payments now made to them to prevent their starvation could be regarded as insurance claims. He therefore proposed that all men of good repute who had worked in the community in whatever line of useful endeavor, whether as machinists, clerks, or bank managers, be regarded as citizen policyholders, having claims against the city in the case of unemployment for fifty dollars a month until such time as they might again be employed. Naturally, he had to talk very slowly and patiently, since the idea was entirely new to his fellow aldermen. But he described his plan as a "straight business proposition," and finally they were persuaded. They worked out the details as to the conditions under which citizens should be regarded as policyholders in the city's social insurance plan to everybody's satisfaction and decided to give checks for fifty dollars a month to the heads of each of B-ville's indigent families.

B-ville's claim adjusters, whose duty it was to investigate the claims of the citizen policyholders, had a much better time than A-town's relief investigators. While the latter had been resentfully regarded as snoopers, the former, having no moral lesson to teach but simply a business transaction to carry out, treated their clients with businesslike courtesy and got the same amount of information as the relief investigators with considerably less difficulty. There were no hard feelings. It further happened, fortunately, that news of B-ville's plans reached a liberal newspaper editor in the big city at the other end of the state. This writer described the plan in a leading feature story headed "B-VILLE LOOKS AHEAD. Great Adventure in Social Pioneering Launched by Upper Valley Community." As a result of this publicity, inquiries about the plan began to come to the city hall even before the first checks were mailed out. This led, naturally, to a considerable feeling of pride on the part of the aldermen, who, being boosters, felt that this was a wonderful opportunity to put B-ville on the map.

Accordingly, the aldermen decided that instead of simply mailing out the checks as they had originally intended, they would publicly present the first checks at a monster civic ceremony. They invited the governor of the state, who was glad to come to bolster his none-too-enthusiastic support in that locality, the president of the state university, the senator from their district, and other functionaries. They decorated the National Guard armory with flags and got out the American Legion Fife and Drum Corps, the Boy Scouts, and other civic organizations. At the big celebration, each family to receive a social insurance check was marched up to the platform to receive it, and the governor and the mayor shook hands with each of them as they came trooping up in their best clothes. Fine speeches were made; there was much cheering and shouting; pictures of the event showing the recipients of the checks shaking hands with the mayor, and the governor patting the heads of the children, were published not only in the local papers but also in several metropolitan picture sections.

Every recipient of these insurance checks had a feeling, therefore, that he had been personally honored, that he lived in a wonderful little town, and that he could face his unemployment with greater courage and assurance, since his community was back of him. The men and women found themselves being kidded in a friendly way by their acquaintances for having been "up there with the big shots," shaking hands with the governor, and so on. The children at school found themselves envied for having had their pictures in the papers. All in all, B-ville's unemployed did not commit suicide, were not haunted by a sense of failure, did not turn to crime, did not get personal maladjustments, did not develop class hatred, as the result of their fifty dollars a month. . . .

At the conclusion of the Professor's story, the discussion began:

"That just goes to show," said the Advertising Man, who was known among his friends as a realistic thinker, "what good promotional work can do. B-ville's city council had real advertising sense, and that civic ceremony was a masterpiece . . . made everyone happy . . . put over the scheme in a big way. Reminds me of the way we do things in our business: as soon as we called horse-mackerel tuna-fish, we developed a big market for it. I suppose if you called relief 'insurance,' you could actually get people to like it, couldn't you?"

"What do you mean, 'calling' it insurance?" asked the Social Worker. "B-ville's scheme wasn't relief at all. It *was* insurance. That's what all such payments should be. What gets me is the stupidity of A-town's city council and all people like them in not realizing that what they call 'relief' is simply the payment of just claims which those unemployed have on a community in a complex interdependent industrial society."

"Good grief, man! Do you realize what you're saying?" cried the

Advertising Man in surprise. "Are you implying that those people had any *right* to that money? All I said was that it's a good idea to *disguise* relief as insurance if it's going to make people any happier. But it's still relief, no matter what you *call* it. It's all right to kid the public along to reduce discontent, but we don't need to kid ourselves as well!"

"But they *do* have a right to that money! They're not getting something for nothing. It's insurance. They did something for the community, and that's their prem—"

"Say, are you crazy?"

"Who's crazy?"

"You're crazy. Relief is relief, isn't it? If you'd only call things by their right names . . ."

"But, confound it, insurance is insurance, isn't it?"

(Since the gentlemen are obviously losing their tempers, it will be best to leave them. The Professor has already sneaked out. When last heard of, not only had the quarrelers stopped speaking to each other, but so had their wives—and the Advertising Man was threatening to disinherit his son if he didn't break off his engagement with the Social Worker's daughter.)

This story has been told not to advance arguments in favor of "social insurance" or "relief" or for any other political and economic arrangement, but simply to show a fairly characteristic sample of language in action. Do the words we use make as much difference in our lives as the story of A-town and B-ville seems to indicate? We often talk about "choosing the right words to express our thoughts," as if thinking were a process entirely independent of the words we think in. But is thinking such an independent process? Do the words we utter arise as a result of the thoughts we have, or are the thoughts we have determined by the linguistic systems we happen to have been taught? The Advertising Man and the Social Worker seem to be agreed that the results of B-ville's program were good, so that we can assume that their notions of what is socially desirable are similar. Nevertheless, they *cannot agree.*

Alfred Korzybski, in his preface to *Science and Sanity* (which discusses many problems similar to those discussed in this book), asks the reader to imagine what the state of technology would be if all lubricants contained emery dust, the presence of which had never been detected. Machines would be short-lived and expensive; the machine age would be a dream of the distant future. If, however, someone were to discover the presence of the emery, we should at once know *in what direction to proceed* in order to release the potentialities of machine power.

Why do people disagree? It isn't a matter of education or intelligence, because quarreling, bitterness, conflict, and breakdown are just as common among the educated as the uneducated, among the clever as the stupid. Human relations are no better among the privileged than the underprivileged. Indeed, well-educated people are often the cleverest in proving that insurance is *really* insurance and that relief is *really* relief—and being well educated they often have such high principles that nothing will make them modify their position in the slightest. Are disagreements then the inevitable results of the nature of human problems and the nature of man? Possibly so—but if we give this answer, we are confessing to being licked before we have even started our investigations.

The student of language observes, however, that it is an extremely rare quarrel that does not involve some kind of *talking*. Almost invariably, before noses are punched or shooting begins, *words are exchanged*—sometimes only a few, sometimes millions. We shall, therefore, look for the "previously undetected emery dust" (or whatever it is that heats up and stops our intellectual machinery) in *language*—that is to say, *our linguistic habits* (how we talk and think and listen) and *our unconscious attitudes toward language*. If we are even partially successful in our search, we may get an inkling of the *direction in which to proceed* in order to release the now imperfectly realized potentialities of human co-operation.

There is a sense in which we all live in two worlds. First, we live in the world of happenings about us which we know at first hand. But this is an extremely small world, consisting only of that continuum of the things that we have actually seen, felt, or heard—the flow of events constantly passing before our senses. So far as this world of personal experience is concerned, Africa, South America, Asia, Washington, New York, or Los Angeles do not exist if we have never been to these places. Chiang Kai-shek is only a name if we have never seen him. When we ask ourselves how much we know at first hand, we discover that we know very little indeed.

Most of our knowledge, acquired from parents, friends, schools, newspapers, books, conversation, speeches, and radio, is received *verbally*. All our knowledge of history, for example, comes to us only in words. The only proof we have that the Battle of Waterloo ever took place is that we have had reports to that effect. These reports are not given us by people who saw it happen, but are based on other reports: reports of reports of reports, which go back ultimately to the first-hand reports given by people who did see it happening. It is through reports, then, and through reports of reports, that we receive most knowledge: about government, about what is happening in China, about what picture is showing at the downtown theater—in fact, about anything which we do not know through direct experience.

Let us call this world that comes to us through words the *verbal world,* as opposed to the world we know or are capable of knowing through our own experience, which we shall call the *extensional world.* (The reason for the choice of the word "extensional" will become clear later.) The human being, like any other creature, begins to make his acquaintance with the extensional world from infancy. Unlike other creatures, however, he begins to receive, as soon as he can learn to understand, reports, reports of reports, reports of reports of reports. In addition he receives inferences made from reports, inferences made from other inferences, and so on. By the time a child is a few years old, has gone to school and to Sunday school, and has made a few friends, he has accumulated a considerable amount of second- and third-hand information about morals, geography, history, nature, people, games—all of which information together constitutes his verbal world.

Now this verbal world ought to stand in relation to the extensional world as a *map* does to the territory it is supposed to represent. If a child grown to adulthood with a verbal world in his head which corresponds fairly closely to the extensional world that he finds around him in his widening experience, he is in relatively small danger of being shocked or hurt by what he finds, because his verbal world has told him what, more or less, to expect. He is prepared for life. If, however, he grows up with a false map in his head—that is, with a head crammed with false knowledge and superstition—he will constantly be running into trouble, wasting his efforts, and acting like a fool. He will not be adjusted to the world as it is; he may, if the lack of adjustment is serious, end up in a mental hospital.

Some of the follies we commit because of false maps in our heads are so commonplace that we do not even think of them as remarkable. There are those who protect themselves from accidents by carrying a rabbit's foot in the pocket. Some refuse to sleep on the thirteenth floor of hotels—this is so common that most big hotels, even in the capitals of our scientific culture, skip "13" in numbering their floors. Some plan their lives on the basis of astrological predictions. Some play fifty-to-one shots on the basis of dream books. Some hope to make their teeth whiter by changing their brand of tooth paste. All such people are living in verbal worlds that bear little, if any, resemblance to the extensional world.

Now, no matter how beautiful a map may be, it is useless to a traveler unless it accurately shows the relationship of places to each other, the structure of the territory. If we draw, for example, a big dent in the outline of a lake for, let us say, artistic reasons, the map is worthless. But if we are just drawing maps for fun without paying any attention to the structure of the region, there is nothing in the world to prevent us from putting in all the extra curlicues and twists we want in the lakes, rivers, and roads. No harm will be done *unless someone tries to plan a trip by such a map.*

Similarly, by means of imaginary or false reports, or by false inferences from good reports, or by mere rhetorical exercises, we can manufacture at will, with language, "maps" which have no reference to the extensional world. Here again no harm will be done unless someone makes the mistake of regarding such "maps" as representing real territories.

We all inherit a great deal of useless knowledge, and a great deal of misinformation and error (maps that were formerly thought to be accurate), so that there is always a portion of what we have been told that must be discarded. But the cultural heritage of our civilization that is transmitted to us—our socially pooled knowledge, both scientific and humane—has been valued principally because we have believed that it gives us accurate maps of experience. The analogy of verbal worlds to maps is an important one . . . It should be noticed at this point, however, that here are two ways of getting false maps of the world into our heads: first, by having them given to us; second, by making them up for ourselves by misreading the true maps given to us.

Reports are verifiable. We may not always be able to verify them ourselves, since we cannot track down the evidence for every piece of history we know, nor can we all go to Evansville to see the remains of the smash-up before they are cleared away. But if we are roughly agreed on the names of things, on what constitutes a "foot," "yard," "bushel," and so on, and on how to measure time, there is relatively little danger of our misunderstanding each other. Even in a world such as we have today, in which everybody seems to be quarreling with everybody else, *we still to a surprising degree trust each other's reports.* We ask directions of total strangers when we are traveling.

We follow directions on road signs without being suspicious of the people who put them up. We read books of information about science, mathematics, automotive engineering, travel, geography, the history of costume, and other such factual matters, and we usually assume that the author is doing his best to tell us as truly as he can what he knows. And we are safe in so assuming most of the time. With the emphasis that is being given today to the discussion of biased newspapers, propagandists, and the general untrustworthiness of many of the communications we receive, we are likely to forget that we still have an enormous amount of reliable information available and that deliberate misinformation, except in warfare, still is more the exception than the rule. The desire for self-preservation that compelled men to evolve means for the exchange of information also compels them to regard the giving of false information as profoundly reprehensible.

At its highest development, the language of reports is the language of science. By "highest development" we mean greatest general usefulness. Presbyterian and Catholic, workingman and capitalist, German and Englishman, *agree* on the meanings of such symbols as $2 \times 2 = 4$, 100° C., HNO_3, 3:35 A.M., 1940 A.D., 5000 r.p.m., 1000 *kilowatts, pulex irritans,* and so on. But how, it may be asked, can there be agreement about even this much among people who are at each other's throats about practically everything else: political philosophies, ethical ideas, religious beliefs, and the survival of my business *versus* the survival of yours? The answer is that circumstances *compel men to agree,* whether they wish to or not. If, for example, there were a dozen different religious sects in the United States, each insisting on its own way of naming the time of the day and the days of the year, the mere necessity of having a dozen different calendars, a dozen different kinds of watches, and a dozen sets of schedules for business hours, trains, and radio programs, to say nothing of the effort that would be required for translating terms from one nomenclature to another, would make life as we know it impossible.

The language of reports, then, including the more accurate reports of science, is "map" language, and because it gives us reasonably accurate representations of the "territory," it enables us to get work done. Such language may often be what is commonly termed "dull" or "uninteresting" reading: one does not usually read logarithmic tables or telephone directories for entertainment. But we could not get along without it. There are numberless occasions in the talking and writing we do in everyday life that *require that we state things in such a way that everybody will agree with our formulation.*

In our suggested writing exercise, judgments are also to be excluded. By judgments, we shall mean *all expressions of the writer's approval or disapproval of the occurrences, persons, or objects he is describing.* For example, a report cannot say, "It was a wonderful car," but must say something like this: "It has been driven 50,000 miles and has never required any repairs." Again statements like "Jack lied to us" must be suppressed in favor of the more verifiable statement, "Jack told us he didn't have the keys to his car with him. However, when he pulled a handkerchief out of his pocket a few minutes later, a bunch of car keys fell out." Also a report may not say, "The senator was stubborn, defiant, and unco-operative," or "The senator courageously stood by his principles"; it must say instead, "The senator's vote was the only one against the bill."

Many people regard statements like the following as statements of "fact": "Jack *lied* to us," "Jerry is a *thief,*" "Tommy is *clever.*" As ordinarily employed, however, the word "lied" involves first an inference (that Jack knew otherwise and deliberately misstated the facts) and secondly a judgment (that the speaker disapproves of what he has inferred that Jack did). In the other two instances, we may substitute such expressions as, "Jerry was convicted of theft and served two years at Waupun," and "Tommy plays the violin, leads his class in school, and is captain of the debating team." After all, to say of a man that he is a "thief" is to say in effect, "He has stolen *and will steal again*"—which is more of a prediction than a report. Even to say, "He has stolen," is to make an inference (and simultaneously to pass a judgment) on an act about which there may be difference of opinion among those who have examined the evidence upon which the conviction was obtained. But to say that he was "convicted of theft" is to make a statement capable of being agreed upon through verification in court and prison records.

Scientific verifiability rests upon the external observation of facts, not upon the heaping up of judgments. If one person says, "Peter is a deadbeat," and another says, "I think so too," the statement has not been verified. In court cases, considerable trouble is sometimes caused by witnesses who cannot distinguish their judgments from the facts upon which those judgments are based. Cross-examinations under these circumstances go something like this:

Witness: That dirty double-crosser Jacobs ratted on me.

Defense Attorney: Your honor, I object.

Judge: Objection sustained. (Witness's remark is stricken from the record.) Now, try to tell the court exactly what happened.

Witness: He double-crossed me, the dirty, lying rat!

Defense Attorney: Your honor, I object!

Judge: Objection sustained. (Witness's remark is again stricken from the record.) Will the witness try to stick to the facts.

Witness: But I'm telling you the facts, your honor. He did double-cross me.

This can continue indefinitely unless the cross-examiner exercises some ingenuity in order to get at the facts behind the judgment. To the witness it is a "fact" that he was "double-crossed." Often hours of patient questioning are required before the factual bases of the judgments are revealed.

Many words, of course, simultaneously convey a report and a judgment on the fact reported . . . For the purposes of a report as here defined, these should be avoided. Instead of "sneaked in," one might say "entered quietly"; instead of "politicians," "congressmen," or "aldermen," or "candidates for office"; instead of "bureaucrat," "public official"; instead of "tramp," "homeless unemployed"; instead of "dictatorial set-up," "centralized authority"; instead of "crackpots," "holders of uncommon views." A newspaper reporter, for example, is not permitted to write, "A crowd of suckers came to listen to Senator Smith last evening in that rickety firetrap and ex-dive that disfigures the south edge of town." Instead he says, "Between seventy-five and a hundred people heard an address last evening by Senator Smith at the Evergreen Gardens near the South Side city limits."

. . . it is important to remember that we are considering language not as an isolated phenomenon, but language in action—language in the full context of the nonlinguistic events which are its setting. The making of noises with the vocal organs is a muscular activity, and like other muscular activities, often involuntary. Our responses to powerful stimuli, such as to something that makes us very angry, are a complex of muscular and physiological events: the contracting of fighting muscles, the increase of blood pressure, change in body chemistry, clutching one's hair, and so on, *and* the making of noises, such as growls and snarls. We are a little too dignified, perhaps, to growl like dogs, but we do the next best thing and substitute a series of words, such as "You dirty double-crosser!" "The filthy scum!"

Similarly, if we are pleasurably agitated, we may, instead of purring or wagging the tail, say things like "She's the sweetest girl in all the world!"

Speeches such as these are, as direct expressions of approval or disapproval, judgments in their simplest form. They may be said to be human equivalents of snarling and purring. "She's the sweetest girl in all the world" is not a statement about the girl; it is a purr. This seems to be a fairly obvious fact; nevertheless, it is surprising how often, when such a statement is made, both the speaker and the hearer feel that something has been said about the girl. This error is especially common in the interpretation of utterances of orators and editorialists in some of their more excited denunciations of "Reds," "greedy monopolists," "Wall Street," "radicals," "our way of life." Constantly, because of the impressive sound of the words, the elaborate structure of the sentences, and the appearance of intellectual progression, we get the feeling that something is being said about something. On closer examination, however, we discover that these utterances merely say, "What I hate ('Reds,' 'Wall Street,' or whatever) I hate very, very much," and "What I like ('our way of life') I like very, very much." We may call such utterances "snarl-words" and "purr-words." They are not reports describing conditions in the extensional world in any way.

To call these judgments "snarl-words" and "purr-words" does not mean that we should simply shrug them off. It means that we should be careful to *allocate the meaning correctly*—placing such a statement as "She's the sweetest girl in the world" as a revelation of the speaker's state of mind, and not as a revelation of facts about the girl. If the "snarl-words" about "Reds," or "greedy monopolists" are accompanied by verifiable reports (which would also mean that we have previously agreed as to who, specifically, is meant by the terms "Reds" or "greedy monopolists"), we might find reason to be just as disturbed as the speaker. If the "purr-words" about the sweetest girl in the world are accompanied by verifiable reports about her appearance, manners, skill in cooking, and so on, we might find reason to admire her too. But "snarl-words" and "purr-words" as such, unaccompanied by reports, offer nothing further to discuss, except possibly the question, "Why do you feel as you do?"

It is usually fruitless to debate such questions as "Was President Roosevelt a great statesman or merely a skillful politician?" "Is the music of Wagner the greatest music of all time or is it merely hysterical screeching?" "Which is the finer sport, tennis or baseball?" "Could

Joe Louis in his prime have licked Bob Fitzsimmons in his prime?" To take sides on such issues of conflicting judgments is to reduce oneself to the same level of stubborn imbecility as one's opponents. But to ask questions of the form, "Why do you like (or dislike) Roosevelt (or Wagner, or tennis or Joe Louis)?" is to learn something about one's friends and neighbors. After listening to their opinions and their reasons for them, we may leave the discussion slightly wiser, slightly better informed, and perhaps slightly less one-sided than we were before the discussion began.

A judgment ("He is a fine boy," "It was a beautiful service," "Baseball is a healthful sport," "She is an awful bore") is a conclusion, summing up a large number of previously observed facts. The reader is probably familiar with the fact that students almost always have difficulty in writing themes of the required length because their ideas give out after a paragraph or two. The reason for this is that those early paragraphs contain so many judgments that there is little left to be said. When the conclusions are carefully excluded, however, and observed facts are given instead, there is never any trouble about the length of papers; in fact, they tend to become too long, since inexperienced writers, when told to give facts, often give far more than are necessary, because they lack discrimination between the important and the trivial.

Still another consequence of judgments early in the course of a written exercise—and this applies also to hasty judgments in everyday thought—is the temporary blindness they induce. When, for example, an essay starts with the words, "He was a real Wall Street executive," or "She was a typical cute little co-ed," if we continue writing at all, we must make all our later statements consistent with those judgments. The result is that all the individual characteristics of this particular "executive" or this particular "co-ed" are lost sight of entirely; and the rest of the essay is likely to deal not with observed facts, but with the writer's private notion (based on previously read stories, movies, pictures, and so forth) of what "Wall Street executives" or "typical co-eds" look like. The premature judgment, that is, often prevents us from seeing what is directly in front of us. Even if the writer feels sure at the beginning of a written exercise that the man he is describing is a "loafer" or that the scene he is describing is a "beautiful residential suburb," he will conscientiously keep such notions out of his head, lest his vision be obstructed.

A few weeks of practice in writing reports, slanted reports, and reports slanted both ways will improve powers of observation, as well as ability to recognize soundness of observation in the writings of others. A sharpened sense for the distinction between facts and judgments, facts and inferences, will reduce susceptibility to the flurries of frenzied public opinion which certain people find it to their interest to arouse. Alarming judgments and inferences can be made to appear inevitable by means of skillfully slanted reports. A reader who is aware of the technique of slanting, however, is relatively difficult to stampede by such methods. He knows too well that there may be other relevant facts which have been left out.

MATHEMATICS AS AN ELEMENT IN THE HISTORY OF THOUGHT*

Alfred North Whitehead

The Science of Pure Mathematics, in its modern developments, may claim to be the most original creation of the human spirit. Another claimant for this position is music. But we will put aside all rivals, and consider the ground on which such a claim can be made for mathematics. The originality of mathematics consists in the fact that in mathematical science connections between things are exhibited which, apart from the agency of human reason, are extremely unobvious. Thus the ideas, now in the minds of contemporary mathematicians, lie very remote from any notions which can be immediately derived by perception through the senses; unless indeed it be perception stimulated and guided by antecedent mathematical knowledge. This is the thesis which I proceed to exemplify.

Suppose we project our imagination backwards through many thousands of years, and endeavour to realise the simple-mindedness of even the greatest intellects in those early societies. Abstract ideas which to us are immediately obvious must have been, for them, matters only of the most dim apprehension. For example take the question of number. We think of the number "five" as applying to appropriate groups of any entities whatsoever—to five fishes, five children, five apples, five days. Thus in considering the relations of the number "five" to the number "three," we are thinking of two groups of things, one with five members and the other with three members. But we are entirely abstracting from any consideration of any particular entities, or even of any particular sorts of entities, which go to make up the membership of either of the two groups. We are merely thinking of those relationships between those two groups which are entirely independent of the individual essences of any of the members of either group. This is a very remarkable feat of abstraction; and it must have taken ages for the human race to rise to it. During a long period, groups of fishes will have been compared to each other in respect to their multiplicity, and groups of days to each other. But the first man who noticed the analogy between a group of seven fishes and a group of seven days made a notable advance in the history of thought. He was the first man who entertained a concept belonging to the science of pure mathematics. At that moment it must have been impossible for him to divine the complexity and subtlety of these abstract mathematical ideas which were waiting for discovery. Nor could he have guessed that these notions would exert a widespread fascination in each succeeding generation. There is an erroneous literary tradition which represents the love of mathematics as a monomania confined to a few eccentrics in each generation. But be this as it may, it would have been impossible to anticipate the pleasure derivable from a type of abstract thinking which had no counterpart in the then-existing society . . . the tremendous future effect of mathematical knowledge on the lives of men, on their daily avocations, on their habitual thoughts, on the organization of society, must have been even more completely shrouded from the foresight of those early thinkers. Even now there is a very wavering grasp of the true position of mathematics as an element in the history of thought. I will not go so far as to say that to construct a history of thought without profound study of the mathematical ideas of successive epochs is like omitting Hamlet from the play which is named after him. That would be claiming too much. But it is certainly analogous to cutting out the part of Ophelia. This simile is singularly very charming—and a little mad. Let us grant that the pursuit of mathematics is a divine madness of the human spirit, a refuge from the goading urgency of contingent happenings.

When we think of mathematics, we have in our mind a science devoted to the exploration of number, quantity, geometry, and in modern times also including investigation into yet more abstract concepts of order, and into analogous types of purely logical relations. The point of mathematics is that in it we have always got rid of the particular instance, and even of any particular sorts of entities. So that for example, no mathematical truths apply merely to fish, or merely to stones, or merely to colours. So long as you are dealing with pure mathematics, you are in the realm of complete and absolute admission that, if any entities whatever have any relations then they must have other relations which satisfy other purely abstract conditions. . . .

The certainty of mathematics depends upon its complete abstract generality. But we can have no *a priori* certainty that we are right in believing that the observed entities in the concrete universe form a particular instance of what falls under our general reasoning. To take another example from arithmetic. It is a general abstract truth of pure mathematics that any group of forty entities can be subdivided into two groups of twenty entities. We are therefore justified in concluding that a particular group of apples which we believe to contain forty members can be subdivided into two groups of apples of which each contains twenty members. But there always remains the possibility that we have miscounted the big group; so that, when we come in practice to subdivide it, we shall find that one of the two heaps has an apple too few or an apple too many. . . .

It is in respect to this process of verification for the particular case that all the trouble arises. In some simple instances, such as the counting of forty apples, we can with a little care arrive at practical certainty. But in general, with more complex instances, complete certainty is unattainable. Volumes, libraries of volumes, have been written on the subject. It is the battle ground of rival philosophers. There are two distinct questions involved. There are particular definite things observed, and we have to make sure that the relations between these things really do obey certain definite exact abstract conditions. There is great room for error here. The exact observational methods of science are all contrivances for limiting these erroneous conclusions as to direct matters of fact. But another question arises. The things directly observed are, almost always, only samples. We want to conclude that the abstract conditions, which hold for the samples, also hold for all other entities which, for some reason or other, appear to us to be of the same sort. This process of reasoning from the sample to the whole species is Induction. The theory of Induction is the despair of philosophy—and yet all our activities are based upon it. Anyhow, in criticising a mathematical conclusion as to a particular matter of fact, the real difficulties consist in finding out the abstract assumptions involved, and in estimating the evidence for their applicability to the particular case in hand. . . .

By comparison with language, we can now see what is the function in thought which is performed by pure mathematics. It is a resolute attempt to go the whole way in the direction of complete analysis, so as to separate the elements of mere matter of fact from the purely abstract conditions which they exemplify. . . .

In a sense, Plato and Pythagoras stand nearer to modern physical science than does Aristotle. The two former were mathematicians, whereas Aristotle was the son of a doctor, though of course he was not thereby ignorant of mathematics. The practical counsel to be derived from Pythagoras, is to measure, and thus to express quality in terms of numerically determined quantity. But the biological sciences, then and till our own time, have been overwhelmingly classificatory. Accordingly, Aristotle by his Logic throws the emphasis on classification. The popularity of Aristotelian Logic retarded the advance of physical science throughout the Middle Ages. If only the schoolmen had measured instead of classifying, how much they might have learnt! . . .

Classification is a halfway house between the immediate concreteness of the individual thing and the complete abstraction of the mathematical notions. The species take account of the specific character, and the genera of the generic character. But in the procedure of relating mathematical notions to the facts of nature, by counting, by measurement, and by geometrical relations, and by types of order, the rational contemplation is lifted from the incomplete abstractions involved in definite species and genera, to the complete abstractions of mathematics. Classification is necessary. But unless you can progress from classification to mathematics, your reasoning will not take you very far. . . .

In the seventeenth century, the birth of modern science required a new mathematics, more fully equipped for the purpose of analysing the characteristics of vibratory existence. And now in the twentieth century we find physicists largely engaged in analysing the periodicities of atoms. Truly, Pythagoras in founding European philosophy and European mathematics, endowed them with the luckiest of lucky guesses—or, was it a flash of divine genius, penetrating to the inmost nature of things?

5

PSYCHOLOGICAL SCIENCE AND OTHER SCIENCES

In some very general ways all sciences—physical, biological, or behavioral—are alike; and together, the sciences contrast sharply with other human approaches to understanding. But each scientific discipline, when viewed more closely, has its own characteristics. Each science may be thought of as an organized social entity, an entity that has its own internal structures and processes, but one that maintains a certain kind of relationship with the larger society in which it exists. Philosophers of science, historians of science, and, in recent years, those who study the sociology of science all have things to say about the distinctive natures of the various sciences and about their interactions with society.

In the following excerpts from an address by Robert Oppenheimer, the noted atomic physicist, the reader can begin to see facets of the sociology of science, and can view some of the differences between psychology and physics.

ANALOGY IN SCIENCE*

Robert Oppenheimer

One would think that the two sciences (physics and psychology) could hardly be further apart. In all hierarchical schemes they are put

* From *American Psychologist,* Vol. 11, No. 3, 1956, pp. 127–135. By permission.

far apart. Psychology, to everyone who works in the field, is felt to be a new subject in which real progress and real objectivity are recent. Physics is, perhaps, as old as the sciences come; physics is reputed to have a large, coherent, connected corpus of certitudes. This does not exist in psychology, and only the beginnings of it, the beginnings of things that are later going to be tied together, are now before us.

But I have always had a feeling that there were ways in which the two sciences had a community; in some sense, of course, all sciences do. One very simple one is that each is responsive to a primitive, permanent, pervasive, human curiosity: what material bodies are and how they behave, on the one hand, and how people and the people-like animals behave and feel and think and learn. These are the curiosities of common life and they will never be abated. Neither, for this reason, can hardly make important pronouncements of a technical sort which do not appear to have some bearing on our views of reality, on metaphysics. Both manifestly have, and continue to have, a fresh and inspiriting effect on the theory of knowledge, on epistemology.

There are other ways in which we are brothers. In the last ten years the physicists have been extraordinarily noisy about the immense powers which, largely through their efforts, but through other efforts as well, have come into the possession of man, powers notably and strikingly for very large-scale and dreadful destruction. We have spoken of our responsibilities and of our obligations to society in terms that sound to me very provincial, because the psychologist can hardly do anything without realizing that for him the acquisition of knowledge opens up the most terrifying prospects of controlling what people do and how they think and how they behave and how they feel. This is true for all of you who are engaged in practice, and as the corpus of psychology gains in certitude and subtlety and skill, I can see that the physicist's pleas that what he discovers be used with humanity and be used wisely will seem rather trivial compared to those pleas which you will have to make and for which you will have to be responsible.

The point, of course, is that as the relevance of what we find to human welfare and human destiny becomes sharper and more manifest, our responsibilities for explication, for explanation, for communication, for teaching grow. These are rather our responsibilities for being sure that we are understood than responsibilities for making decisions; they are our responsibilities for laying the basis in understanding for these decisions.

There are other ways in which we are alike. The practical usefulness of our professions gives us often the impression that we are right for the wrong reasons, and that our true nature is very different from our public presence. We are both faced with the problem of the need to keep intact the purity of academic and abstract research and, at the same time, to nourish and be nourished by practice. In physics, of course, our debt to technology and engineering is unlimited. I think it would be so in psychology as well.

Both sciences, all sciences, arise as refinements, corrections, and adaptations of common sense. There are no unique, simple, scientific methods that one can prescribe; but there are certainly traits that any science must have before it pretends to be one. One is the quest for objectivity. I mean that not in a metaphysical sense; but in a very practical sense, as the quest to be sure that we understand one another, and that all qualified practitioners mean essentially the same thing. Common-sense language is inherently ambiguous; when the poet uses it, or the rhetorician, he exploits the ambiguity, and even when we talk in ordinary life we almost need ambiguity in order to get by. But in science we try to get rid of that, we try to talk in such simple terms, and match our talk with deeds in such a way that we may differ as to facts, but we can resolve the differences. This is, of course, the first step in the quest for certitude. But certitude is not the whole story. When we move from common sense into scientific things, we also move toward generality using analysis, using observation and, in the end, using experiment. And we also do something which is even more characteristic; we look for novelty, we look for transcendence, we look for features of experience that are not available in ordinary life. Characteristic in physics are the instruments that enable us to transcend elementary, daily experience: the telescope that lets us look deep into the sky, the enormous accelerators which are, today, the logical extension of the microscope, enabling us to look on a finer and finer scale into the structure of matter.

I need to be cautious in citing parallels in psychology; but certainly the use of hypnosis, the use of drugs, are typical extensions into unfamiliar realms of human experience which just bring out characteristics of psychological phenomena that are largely lost in day-to-day experience. There is an example which may be only a physicist's idea of a perfect experiment. It is the work that was done at McGill in the last years on the effects of reducing sensory stimuli, with very simple arrangements to change the level of stimulation; these produce most striking and almost frighteningly great, though essentially temporary, changes in memory, in the intellectual and cognitive life of the subjects. This is again an example of carrying to an extreme something which is indeed encountered in ordinary experience but which only the patience and the abstractness of experimental enquiry is likely to make manifest.

We come from common sense; we work for a long time; then we give back to common sense refined, original, and strange notions, and enrich what men know and how they live. And here, I suppose, the real hero is the teacher. . . .

But for all of that I would like to say something about what physics has to give back to common sense that it seemed to have lost from it, not because I am clear that these ideas are important tools in psychological research, but because it seems to me that the worst of all possible misunderstandings would be that psychology be influenced to model itself after a physics which is not there any more, which has been quite outdated.

We inherited, say at the beginning of this century, a notion of the physical world as a causal one, in which every event could be accounted for if we were ingenious, a world characterized by number, where everything interesting could be measured and quantified, a determinist world, a world in which there was no use or room for individuality, in which the object of study was simply there and how you studied it did not affect the object, it did not affect the kind of description you gave of it, a world in which objectifiability went far beyond merely our own agreement on what we meant by words and what we are talking about, in which objectification was meaningful irrespective of any attempt to study the system under consideration. It was just the given real object; there it was, and there was nothing for you to worry about of an epistemological character. This extremely rigid picture left out a great deal of common sense. I do not know whether these missing elements will prove helpful; but at least their return may widen the resources that one can bring to any science.

What are these ideas? In our natural, unschooled talk, and above all in unschooled talk about psychological problems, we have five or six things which we have got back into physics with complete rigor, with complete objectivity, in the sense that we understand one another, with a complete lack of ambiguity and with a perfectly phenomenal technical success. One of them is just this notion that the physical world is not completely determinate. There are predictions you can make about it but they are statistical; and any event has in it the nature of the surprise, of the miracle, of something that you could not figure out. Physics is predictive, but within limits; its world is ordered, but not completely causal.

Another of these ideas is the discovery of the limits on how much we can objectify without reference to what we are really talking about in an operational, practical sense. We can say the electron has a certain charge and we do not have to argue as to whether we are looking at it to say that; it always does. We cannot say it has a place or a motion. If we say that we imply something about what we ourselves —I do not mean as people but as physicists—are doing about it.

A third point is very closely related to this; it is the inseparability of what we are studying and the means that are used to study it, the organic connection of the object with the observer. Again, the observer is not in this case a human, but in psychology the observer sometimes is a human.

And then, as logical consequences of this, there is the idea of totality, or wholeness. Newtonian physics, classical science, was differential; anything that went on could be broken up into finer and finer elements and analyzed so. If one looks at an atomic phenomenon between the beginning and the end, the end will not be there; it will be a different phenomenon. Every pair of observations taking the form "we know this, we then predict that" is a global thing; it cannot be broken down.

Finally, every atomic event is individual. It is not, in its essentials, reproducible.

This is quite a pack of ideas that we always use: individuality, wholeness, the subtle relations of what is seen with how it is seen, the indeterminacy and the acausality of experience. And I would only say that if physics could take all these away for three centuries and then give them back in ten years, we may well say that all ideas that occur in common sense are fair as starting points, not guaranteed to work but perfectly valid as the material of the analogies with which we start.

The whole business of science does not lie in getting into realms which are unfamiliar in normal experience. There is an enormous work of analyzing, of recognizing similarities and analogies, of getting the feel of the landscape, an enormous qualitative sense of family relations, of taxonomy. It is not always tactful to try to qualify; it is not always clear that by measuring one has found something very much worth measuring. It is true that for the Babylonians it was worth measuring—noting—the first appearances of the moon because it had a practical value. Their predictions, their prophecies, and their magic would not work without it; and I know that many psychologists have the same kind of reason for wanting to measure. It is a real property of the real world that you are measuring, but it is not necessarily the best way to advance true understanding of what is going on; and I would make this very strong plea for pluralism with regard to methods that, in the necessarily early stages of sorting out an immensely vast experience, may be fruitful and may be helpful. They may be helpful not so much for attaining objectivity, nor for a quest for certitude which will never be quite completely attained. But there is a place for the use of naturalistic methods, the use of descriptive methods. I have been immensely impressed by the work of one man who visited us last year at the Institute, Jean Piaget. When you look at his work, his statistics really consist of one or two cases. It is just a start; and yet I think he has added greatly to our understanding. It is not that I am sure he is right, but he has given us something worthy of which to enquire whether it is right; and I make this plea not to treat too harshly those who tell you a story, having observed carefully without having established that they are sure that the story is the whole story and the general story.

It is of course in that light that I look at the immense discipline of practice, that with all its pitfalls, with all the danger that it leads to premature and incorrect solutions, does give an incredible amount of experience. Physics would not be where it is, psychology would not be where it is if there were not a great many people willing to pay us for thinking and working on their problems. . . .

If any of this is true there is another thing that physicists and psychologists have in common: we are going to have quite a complicated life. The plea for a plural approach to exploration, the plea for a minimal definition of objectivity that I have made, means that we are going to learn a terrible lot; there are going to be many different ways of talking about things; the range from almost un-understood practice to recondite and abstract thought is going to be enormous. It means there are going to have to be a lot of psychologists, as there are getting to be a lot of physicists. When we work alone trying to get something straight it is right that we be lonely; and I think in the really decisive thoughts that advance a science loneliness is an essential part. . . . When we are trying to do something practical it is nice to have an excess of talent, to have more sailors than are needed to sail the ship and more cooks than are needed to cook the meal; the reason is that in this way a certain elegance, a certain proper weighing of alternatives, guides the execution of the practical task.

We are, for all kinds of reasons, worrying about how our scientific community is to be nourished and enough people who are good enough are to come and work with us. And then on the other side we are worried about how we are to continue to understand one another, and not get totally frustrated by the complexity and immensity of our enterprises.

I think there are good reasons of an inherent kind, beside the competitive compulsion of the communist world, why we would do well to have more and better scientists. I know that exhortation, money, patronage, will do something about this; but I do not think that is all that will be needed. I think that if we are to have some success it must be because, as a part of our culture, the understanding, the life of the mind, the life of science, in itself, as an end as well as a means, is appreciated, is enjoyed, and is cherished. I think that has to be a very much wider thing in the community as a whole, if we are to enjoy with the community as a whole the healthy relations without which the developing powers of scientific understanding, prediction, and control are really monstrous things.

It may not be so simple, to have in the community at large some genuine experience of the pleasures of understanding and discovery. It may not be simple because what this requires is not merely that this experience be agreeable, but that it have a touch of virtue; that not only the consideration of ends, of products, of accomplishments and status, but the texture of life itself, its momentary beauty and its nobility, be worth some attention; and that among the things that contribute to these be the life of the mind and the life of science. Let us try to make it so.

6

A PSYCHOLOGICAL SCIENTIST

The appreciation of any science can be enhanced by an intimate knowledge of some of the individuals who advance it. Every scientist strives for great impersonality while plying his trade, while uncovering, reporting, and interpreting data; and science in general is characterized by its formal rules and procedures for ensuring objective, impersonal observations. But the scientist himself remains a person. He has flesh, blood, motives, aspirations, imagination, fallibility. His attributes as a human individual surely have a bearing on the nature of the problems he chooses to attack, on the style with which he conducts his intellectual life, and perhaps on the kind of interpretation he puts upon his data. Questions concerning these and related matters may profitably be kept in mind while reading the following excerpt from the autobiography of Edward Chace Tolman, a very distinguished psychologist who, by the time of his death in 1959, had lived through a considerable proportion of the history of the young discipline he chose to enter.

HISTORY OF PSYCHOLOGY IN AUTOBIOGRAPHY*

Edward Chace Tolman

I was born in Newton, Massachusetts in 1886. I went to the Newton Public Schools, which were then, and still are, considered to be unusually good, and then went to the Massachusetts Institute of Tech-

* Excerpted from Edward Chace Tolman, *History of Psychology in Autobiography,* Vol. IV. Worcester, Mass.: Clark University Press, 1952. Pp. 323–331, 335–339. By permission.

nology, where I obtained a B.S. in electrochemistry in 1911. I went to M.I.T. not because I wanted to be an engineer, but because I had been good in mathematics and science in high school and because of family pressure. After graduating from Technology I became more certain of my own wants and transferred to Harvard for graduate work in philosophy and psychology.

My family was, I suppose, what now would be called "upper middle" or possibly "lower upper." My father was president of a manufacturing company and my maternal uncle president of a similar company. My brother, who was five years older, and I were, first one and then the other, expected to go into our father's business. Hence, we both went to M.I.T.; my father had been a member of the first graduating class and was a Trustee. My brother, however, escaped by becoming a theoretical chemist and physicist and I, having read some William James during my senior year at Technology, fancied that I wanted to become a philosopher. Upon graduating from M.I.T., I went to the Harvard summer school and took an introductory course in philosophy with Perry and one in psychology with Yerkes—both then young assistant professors in the combined department of philosophy and psychology. I decided then and there that I did not have brains enough to become a philosopher (that was still the day of great metaphysical systems), but that psychology was nearer my capacities and interests. It offered, at that date, what seemed a nice compromise between philosophy and science.

The fact that my brother and I both avoided family expectations and chose academic careers, instead of going into the factory, and the further fact that this led to no family quarrels and that we were even financially supported during the process, probably tells a good deal about the nature of the family setup and of the general cultural milieu in which we lived. Our immediate family consisted of a warm, loving, but in some areas Puritanical mother and of a kindly, affectionate but very much occupied father—who was depressingly energetic and excited about his business, so much so that when he tried to get us boys interested in it he merely wore us out—and of a still older sister who, as far as I was concerned, was already leading a grown-up life outside my ken. This seems the sort of setup which the recent studies of ethnocentrism suggest may be conducive to the developing of ambitious, but non-authoritarian personalities. Although we lived in a well-to-do conventional suburb with stress on appearances, there still persisted in our family and in those of some of the neighbors the legacy of reformism, equal rights for Negroes, women's rights, Unitarianism and humanitarianism from the earlier days of the "Flowering of New England." These social tendencies were combined with the special Bostonian emphasis on "culture" together with, in our family, a special dose of moral uplift and pacifism. Typical mottoes of my father were, on the one hand, "Tend to business" and, on the other, "Man does not live by bread alone." There was relatively great freedom of discussion between children and parents and close ties to the wider family. What I am trying to say is that the rebellion of my brother and of myself against parental domination was in directions which the parents themselves could not too greatly, or too consciously, disapprove. We were choosing the professions. We were set to increase the sum of human knowledge and presumably were to apply such an increase of knowledge to the betterment of mankind. Furthermore, we would be living up to the Puritan tradition of hard work and to the Quaker tradition, on our mother's side, of plain living and high thinking. This is not to say that our parents were not deeply and basically disappointed that we did not really adopt the other strain in their own natures and in the New England culture at large—that of making money and taking advantage of the expanding national economy. But it *is* to say that, since in large measure we were merely following what they had preached, they could not show their disappointment too strongly either to themselves or to us. Undoubtedly this typical parent-child tragedy of America was mitigated for them, as it is for so many American parents, because we, the children, were striving towards what, at least in New England, could be considered a form of upward social mobility.

Turn now to a more particular question. Why did I, personally, go into psychology rather than choosing to follow my brother into physics or chemistry. I suspect the following factors were involved. First, during adolescence it seems to have been my brother with whom I identified and picked as my model rather than my father. Thus, I was set to follow my brother into the academic world. On the other hand, I did not dare compete with him in his own field. An older brother is both a tremendous example and a very frightening rival who, because of his advantage in years, has one licked intellectually before one starts. Secondly, I suspect that, although I was considered by my teachers to be as good as my brother in mathematics and science, my mind was in fact less rigorous and less logical. Third, as the youngest in the family I had been over-babied and over-protected—being made into a shy adolescent—who had therefore been led, perhaps, to become especially sensitive to and interested in human relations. Further, at the age of seventeen I was taken out of school for two years because of a functional heart disorder which at that time was laid to too rapid physical growth; the more probable psychoanalytic explanation I leave to the reader. This left me much time to introspect, to become somewhat morbid and to imagine myself as a potential "writer," "humanitarian," or "saver-of-souls"—in, of course, a chaste, rationalistic, Unitarian sort of way. Again, as a late maturer and one who had always been poor at sports and one who, no doubt due to the influences of a mother of Quaker origin, was afraid of bodily competition and of masculinity in general, I probably had suffered a sufficient number of rejections from all but a small intimate group of boyhood friends to have had another reason for needing to "understand" human reactions. Although I had thought I wanted to be a philosopher, I can remember the excitement I felt in that first course in psychology with Yerkes in which we did little "experiments" on reaction time, mental images, and the like. I felt that here one was going to learn what made people tick. It would be much more successful than preaching at them. (I had gone through a phase of thinking that I wanted to be a Unitarian minister.)

In the fall of 1911, therefore, after only one summer session course in philosophy and one in psychology, I began at Harvard as a full graduate student (unthinkable in these days) in the joint department of philosophy and psychology. The courses I remember most vividly were: Perry's course in Ethics, which laid the basis for my later interest in motivation and, indeed, gave me the main concepts (reinforced by a reading of McDougall's *Social Psychology* as part of the requirement of the course) which I have retained ever since; Holt's course in Experimental (largely two-point thresholds and epicritic and protopathic sensations) which I took my first semester and which proved a terrible letdown from the really humanly important problems which I had supposed psychology was to be concerned with; Langfeld's course in Advanced General, using Titchener as a textbook, which almost sold me temporarily on structuralistic introspectionism; Holt's seminar in Epistemology in which I was introduced to, and excited by, the "New Realism"; and Yerkes' course in Comparative, using Watson's *Behavior—an Introduction to Comparative Psychology,* which was just out, as a text.

In addition to these more or less formal courses there was the graduate research done under Münsterberg with Langfeld doing most of the actual supervision. This, if I remember correctly, I began after one year only of graduate enrollment. It had, of course, a tremendous influence upon me. Münsterberg was then at the height of his interest in applied psychology. And most of the research projects which were being carried out in the laboratory involved primarily objective measurements of sensory-motor skills. And even my own research dissertation, which was assigned to me, and which involved the learning and relearning of nonsense syllables under pleasant and unpleasant odors, according to Ebbinghaus's Learning and Savings Method, was primarily objective in nature. I used the then up-to-date *"Rupp-Lippmann Gedächtnis Apparat"* and all I had to do was to sit and count revolutions. Yet in spite of this objective character of practically all of the research being carried out and reported in the weekly laboratory meetings, Münsterberg several times made little opening speeches to the effect that *the* method of psychology was *introspection.* We were expected to ask our subjects, the other graduate students in the group, for introspections, and we took these introspections down in our protocols. But, as far as I remember, none of us was able to make much use of them in his final write-up. And this troubled my theoretical mind. If introspection were "the" method of psychology and we weren't doing it, shouldn't I really go to Cornell where Titchener taught one to do it properly? This worry about introspection is perhaps one reason why my introduction in Yerkes' course to Watson's behaviorism came as a tremendous stimulus and relief. If objective measurement of behavior and not introspection was the true method of psychology I didn't have to worry any longer that we were not doing the latter, or, at least, not doing it in any consistent and approved way.

I say that this was a great relief to my "theoretical mind." As to just when and why this theoretical orientation developed I am not clear. It may be in part constitutional, whatever that may mean. But I am more inclined to believe that it developed from my early fear of, and awkwardness in, manipulatory activities; I had never been especially good in the laboratory at M.I.T. Such fear and awkwardness were perhaps induced as a reaction against my father's extreme interest and proficiency in such matters and also against my brother's slightly greater identification with our father's pattern.

Whatever the explanation, I have always wanted simple and wide-reaching, if not too precise, explanations and have always bogged down in the face of a multiplicity of facts. I can learn facts if I have to, but I forget them equally easily. And in any argument, academic or otherwise, I always find myself handicapped by having forgotten the factual details which alone would buttress my stand. I can make a parade of scholarship, but I find it tiresome and the parade is, I suspect, usually a phony. All the necessary facts are just too many for me to keep in mind. I suspect that I also have some weakness, innate or acquired, in verbal imagery. This is the reason I feel comfortable only when I have translated my explanatory arguments into diagrams. I always did like curves better than equations. Analytical geometry was a lot more fun than advanced algebra. (They used to be separate courses in my day.) I am very unhappy whenever I do not have a blackboard in my office.

At the end of my first graduate year at Harvard I went to Germany for the summer to help me prepare for the required Ph.D. examination in German. I have always been enormously intrigued by foreign languages although I have no natural talent for them. For I have a poor ear and always have to learn phrases and vocabulary by seeing the words and not just by hearing them. At Langfeld's suggestion, I spent a month in Giessen with Koffka, who had been a fellow student of Langfeld's in Berlin and who was then a young *Privatdozent* in psychology at the University of Giessen, and so got my first introduction to Gestalt psychology—although at that time I sensed only vaguely what it was all about. Nevertheless it prepared me to be receptive to Gestalt concepts when after the first World War we began hearing about them more fully in this country through the writings of Wertheimer, Köhler and Koffka. And in the fall of 1923 I went back to Giessen for a couple of months to learn more.

After getting my doctor's degree at Harvard in 1915 I was instructor for three years at Northwestern. I had a compulsive drive from the beginning to do research and to write. I think this was due in part to my brother's example, who was already hell-bent on research and academic success. This compulsion for research and writing, although it did not result in a very large output at the time, interfered with my learning to become much of a teacher. I was still relatively self-conscious and inarticulate, and was afraid of my classes. Also my difficulty in—or dislike for—organizing and remembering a large array of facts was already a handicap. Further, this was just before we got into the first World War and my pacifist training, plus my own problems about aggression, kept me in a terrific emotional turmoil so that I did a still poorer job. I was called before the Dean sometime during the winter of 1917–18 because I had given my name to a student publication, circulated in the Middle West, that was concerned with "war aims," and which had, no doubt, something of a pacifist tinge. The Dean, in leafing through an issue in my presence did not feel any less hostile because the leading article turned out to be by no less eminent a person than David Starr Jordan. In any event, I was dismissed at the end of that academic year on the grounds of war retrenchment and my not too successful teaching. But I have always thought that my near pacifism had something to do with it. I escaped the first draft by being a couple of months too old. But the second draft came along and my pacifist principles and my doubts about the war did not prevent me from signing up and trying to get a commission. But I was already too late to get into the psychological testing service organized by Yerkes. In the early fall of 1918 I was offered a commission to work with Dunlap and Stratton on the screening of air force candidates. But by that time everyone knew that the Armistice was on its way. So I did not accept.

In the meantime, during the summer of 1918, I was without a job but by luck plus Langfeld's good offices I was offered in the fall an instructorship at California. And here in Berkeley I have stayed extremely happy ever since until very recently. From the very first California symbolized for me some sort of a final freeing from my overwhelmingly too Puritanical and too Bostonian upbringing. The "Freedom of the West," whether real or fancied, at once captured my imagination and my loyalty and has claimed them ever since—although with the years I have, of course, become aware that all is not gold that glitters—even in California. In any case, there are features about the climate and the landscape which seem to me better as a steady diet than those provided by any other place in the world. Particularly the Bay Area (although it produces its share of tonsils, allergies, and influenzas) seems absolutely ideal as an all-year-round working climate. Whatever my increasing psychological maturity—and there has been some—I like to credit most of it to the social, intellectual, and physical virtues of Berkeley plus an extraordinarily happy marriage.

I have never been comfortable or efficient in administrative or committee activities and have in large part managed to escape them. My drive has gone into trying to be creative and in my earlier years whenever I was feeling inept on some social or academic occasion, I can remember going home and talking to myself in some such words as: "Well, I'll show them, I will be better known in my field than they will be in theirs." And then I would return to the laboratory, or the study, with an enhanced drive. This compulsive academic ambition, which has, of course, lessened with the years—this self-ideal of someone going to be truly successful in the academic world—came, I suppose, from the fact that in childhood and boyhood I was always successful in school, but never on the playground, and from the fact that, as already indicated, I identified with my older brother. Furthermore, Academe was for me a protected haven in which one could release one's aggressions, of which I undoubtedly have my share, and stick one's neck out on paper without its being too obvious either to oneself or to the other fellow.

Having thus tried to think out, as a very amateur clinical psychologist, what kind of a person I think I am and how I think I got that way, let me try to present a brief history of my psychological interests and concepts. Presumably these have been affected by the structure of my personality; but whatever the interconnections, these are beyond my ability to unravel. I shall present now, therefore, merely as objective and straightforward an account of my ideas as I can.

In my three beginning years as instructor at Northwestern I was still thinking largely in terms of classical introspective and associationistic problems. For, although I had been, as I said, tremendously excited by Yerkes' introduction to and criticism of Watson's behaviorism, the behavioristic point of view had not yet really got into my blood. Thus the first papers I turned out were concerned with such pre-behavioristic problems as retroactive inhibition, imageless thought, and association times for pleasant, unpleasant and neutral words.

When, however, I joined the department at Berkeley as instructor in 1918, I found it was up to me to suggest a new course. Remembering Yerkes' course and Watson's textbook I proposed "comparative psychology." And it was this that finally launched me down the behavioristic slope. Only a few students enrolled and at first a lot of time was spent in arguing against anthropomorphism and the Clever Hans error. But, before too long, I actually acquired some rats from the Long-Evans strain which had been developed in the Anatomy Department. And I and a few graduate, or advanced undergraduate, students began trying out minor experiments in learning. (Even though I had been clumsy in the physical and chemical laboratories at M.I.T., I *could* build mazes.)

It was Watson's denial of the Law of Effect and his emphasis on Frequency and Recency as the prime determiners of animal learning which attracted our attention. In this we were on Watson's side. But we got ourselves—or at least I got myself—into a sort of in-between position. On the one hand I sided with Watson in not liking the Law of Effect. But, on the other hand, I also did not like Watson's oversimplified notions of stimulus and of response. Nor did I like his treatment of each single stimulus and each single response as a quite insulated phenomenon which has practically no relation to any other stimuli or any other responses. That is, I was already becoming influenced by Gestalt psychology and conceived that a rat in running a maze must be learning a lay-out or pattern and not just having connections between atom-like stimuli and atom-like responses "stamped in" or "stamped out," whether by exercise *or* by effect. In fact, my objection to Thorndike's Law of Effect was not to the importance of motivation as a factor in learning, but rather to his wholly mechanical notion as to its operation by way of effect. According to Thorndike, an animal learned, not because it achieved a wanted goal by a certain series of responses, but merely because a quite irrelevant "pleasantness" or "unpleasantness" was, so to speak, shot at it, as from a squirt gun, after it had reached the given goal-box or gone into the given *cul de sac*. And it is this same quite mechanical and irrelevant notion as to the operation of the modern successor of Effect—"Reinforcement"—which underlies, I believe, my main objection to *it*. I have, that is, always found difficulty in conceiving how a completely post and divorced "pleasantness," or a completely post and divorced "need-reduction" (i.e., reinforcement), can act back upon and selectively strengthen the appropriate synaptic connections merely because these synapses happen, quite irrelevantly, to have been the ones which have functioned most recently in time.

It was also during this early period at California that I began developing certain more basic theoretical concepts. These were initiated by a growing belief that a really useful behaviorism would not be a mere "muscle-twitchism" such as Watson's. It soon appeared to me that "responses," as significant for psychology, are defined not by their physiological, muscular or glandular, details but rather by the sort of rearrangements between organisms and environment or between the organism and its own internal states which they achieve. It also seemed to me that "stimuli" as actually used by psychologists are defined in most cases not in terms of the details of sense organ stimulation but in terms of environmental "objects" and "situations" identifiable only in relatively gross, often merely commonsense, terms. That is, I was beginning to have the as yet rather vague notion that there was something which I wanted to call "behavior *qua* behavior." This would be something other than and different from the mere contractions and gland secretions and the mere punctiform sense-organ stimuli underlying such behavior.

The further notion that purpose and cognition are essential descriptive ingredients of any such non-physiologically defined "behavior *qua* behavior" I borrowed from Perry. He pointed out that behavior as such is both persistent and docile. (Thorndike's cat exhibited persistence and docility relative to getting out of the box.) The cat's behavior has to be described and identified in terms of these purposive and cognitive features—but in a quite non-metaphysical and non-teleological sense.

During this period I also spent considerable effort in trying to translate some of the familiar pre-behavioral concepts, such as "sensation," "emotion," "ideas" and "consciousness," into these new, non-physiological behavioral terms. And in the course of so doing I came to use the term "molar" to designate "behavior *qua* behavior," as contrasted with the term "molecular" to designate the underlying physiological units of sense-organ stimulation, central neural activity and final muscle contraction or gland secretion. This pair of terms—"molar" vs. "molecular"—was suggested to me by Professor Donald C. Williams, then a graduate student in philosophy and psychology in Berkeley.

The above ideas, expanded and elaborated, were finally brought together in the book, *Purposive Behavior in Animals and Men* (1932). As I survey now ambivalently that extensive tome, I find a number of features in it which strike me as probably still worth calling attention to.

I would like to turn now to some of the kinds of experiments on rat learning done in the Berkeley laboratory which seem to have influenced, or been influenced by, my theoretical position. Theory is viable and to be justified only in so far as it stimulates, or is stimulated by, research. My theoretical pronouncements have, to be sure, usually been phrased merely loosely and programmatically. And so they have seldom made possible any precise theoretical deductions which could then be specifically subjected to experimental test. Nevertheless, these theoretical meanderings have conditioned me and my students to be interested in certain *kinds* of *experiment*. The theory though loose, has been fertile; perhaps fertile primarily because loose.

Now, for the experiments themselves. In trying some two years ago to summarize the major directions of research in the Berkeley laboratory it seemed to me that a majority of the experiments could be grouped under five main headings: (1) "latent learning," (2) "vicarious trial and error" (VTE), (3) "searching for the stimulus," (4) "hypotheses in rats" and (5) "spatial orientation." I shall not attempt to catalogue these experiments here nor shall I attempt to give the credit which is due to the individual students and research workers who actually had most of the specific ideas, developed the experimental designs, and did the actual work. Rather, I wish to suggest merely that all of the experiments were in one way or another supportive, on the one hand, of a field theory of rat learning, and, on the other hand, of a theory which asserts that the animal brings to the stimulus situation certain cognitive sets—"hypotheses," means-end-readiness; needs to solve—VTE's and searching for the stimulus—as well as specific states of motivation. These cognitive sets and motivational states cause him to react selectively and actively to the then and there presented stimulus array and determine the behavior space which he comes to perceive and the new means-end-readiness (belief-value matrices) which he will carry away. All of these experiments from my point of view, if not from that of their authors, have reinforced the general notion of the essentially cognitive character of learning. The original crucial experiments in this doctrine of the cognitive character of learning were those on "latent learning" initiated by Blodgett.

Turn now to a quite different problem. I have always been obsessed by a need for a single comprehensive theory or scheme for the whole of psychology. And I have also always wanted to be something more than a mere learning or rat psychologist. I have wanted a scheme which would cover not only rat learning but also one which would be pertinent to the problems of human thought and of human motivation. In *Purposive Behavior in Animals and Men* I was already tempted into pronunciamentos concerning primary and secondary drives, demands, insight and ideation as well as concerning learning *per se*. And under the impetus of a general human concern for social events and of a need to discover how man is ever to achieve a stable, or even a merely satisfying, society I have a number of times been tempted into relatively *ad hoc* assertions concerning drives or needs and concerning complex motivational dynamisms both in individuals and in society.

All of these pronouncements have been somewhat abortive because of lack of training on my part in the other social sciences and even in personality psychology and in social psychology. Yet I do not wish to disown them. The pronouncements may have been naive; but I do not think that any of them has been basically wrong or mischievous. They constituted my first steps towards a more complete conceptual scheme—a scheme which would allow me to handle not only simple learning but also problems such as the operation of innate or socially acquired secondary and tertiary needs, the operation of the psychoanalytical and other dynamisms, and finally, the explanation and prevention of individual and social maladjustments. I have been concerned throughout with man's basic needs, biological or social, and with the question of how these needs become modified through social learning as a result of given cultures and given training procedures within a family. Why is it that individuals and cultures go astray? Why is it that a social system seems so seldom to allow for reasonable satisfactions in most of the individuals involved in it? Can we arrive at some naturalistic definitions of the good life or of different kinds of good life? And, having arrived at such definitions, can psychology and the social sciences eventually agree upon ways to produce such lives? These are the sorts of questions which I would seek to raise and would like answers for.

Very recently I have attempted a new theoretical statement, more comprehensive, I believe, than that presented in *Purposive Behavior in Animals and Men* (1932) which I hope eventually may allow for the putting and answering of such questions in a fruitful way. Let me give a brief résumé of this new scheme. I now find it useful to postulate three main systems of intervening variables: a need-system, a belief-value matrix or matrices, and concrete behavior spaces. This is not the place for an extended exposition of these constructs. I wish merely to indicate their general character.

The need-system. This construct is patterned on Lewin's concept of the inner core of the psychological person as composed of intercommunicating need and quasi-need compartments. Instead of postulating, as I have formerly, two different kinds of needs—positive needs and negative needs—I now assume that each need has both its positive and its negative side. I assume, for example, that food-hunger, when aroused, is operationally definable both as a readiness to approach and eat foods and as a readiness to avoid and to get away from non-foods. And, likewise, I assume that fear, when aroused, is operationally definable both as a readiness to avoid and/or get away from painful situations and as a readiness to get to and to remain in "safe," "secure" situations. To define operationally the magnitude of the arousal of any given need at a given time one will have to agree upon a "standard" defining, positive or negative, situation in which the magnitudes of the approach, or avoidance, responses can be quantitatively measured. Such defining experiments will not be easy ones to decide upon; nor will they be technically easy to carry out.

But the notion of such possible experiments is, I believe, implicit in almost everyone's thinking about needs.

This construct of a need system is accompanied also by an assertion that a distinction is to be drawn between such *needs,* as measurable behavioral propensities, to go to or away from such and such types of goal objects and the *physiological drive states* which are often determinative of these needs. Physiological drive states are an independent variable; needs are an intervening variable. This distinction between physiological drive states and needs allows for such facts, for example, as that food-hunger, as *drive state,* defined as a condition of physiological deprivation, and food-hunger, as *need,* defined as a behavioral readiness to approach and consume food, are not necessarily related in linear fashion. The concept of need compartments also allows for the assumption that some of the tension in a compartment may under some conditions be aroused directly by an environmental stimulus situation in some degree independently of the presence, or absence, of a correlated physiological drive state. Finally, the construct of a system of intercommunicating compartments suggests the possibility of hierarchies of superordination and subordination among needs and of mutual facilitations or inhibitions between needs.

Belief-value matrices. This construct, as has been indicated, is a development of the earlier concept of means-end-readiness. Belief-value matrices are thought of as chains of beliefs (means-end-readinesses) which connect successive banks of types of objects to one another in means-end, instrumental, fashion. Such means-end beliefs include also the characters of the "types of behavior" to be performed if the given type of means is to lead to the given type of end. And each categorized bank of objects, whether functioning as means or as end, is to be conceived as constituting a kind of generalization dimension along which are located functionally similar sub-types of object. Any given matrix may thus be thought of as in the nature of a pattern of "platonic ideas" (i.e., object-type differentiations, behavior-type differentiations and generalizations plus means-end relationships). Finally, there are also present in a matrix positive or negative values (deriving from the aroused needs), deposited on types of ends and relayed back to the means and which will be distributed along the generalization dimensions.

Finally, any matrix with its differentiations, generalizations, beliefs and values is activated by the aroused needs and the present stimulus situation and serves along with the presented environmental stimuli, to determine the character of the specific concrete "behavior space" which will be "perceived" at the moment.

The behavior space. This third construct is very similar to Lewin's Life Space save that the "insides" of Lewin's "psychological person" have been elaborated and placed outside as the need system and the governing belief-value matrix. The behavior space contains a "behaving self" which is perceived as located in time and place relative to the perceived array of objects and possible locomotions. The behaving self contains within itself merely one or more negative "need-pushes" (not complete needs). These need-pushes are derived from the needs and functions in that, as negative, they cause the behaving person to be attracted to positive valences and repelled by negative valences. The valences themselves are derived from the values in the governing belief-value matrix. Values are for given *types* of object. Valences are for concrete *instances* of such types of object. Lastly, it may be emphasized that, in the case of human organisms, the self, both as behaving self and as possible goal selfs, will appear in practically any behavior space.

The just preceding paragraphs are, I realize, too condensed and the model itself is too complicated for such a brief account to have much intelligibility. I have introduced it, partly, to indicate that I am still up to my old trick of trying to talk about too many facts and findings at once, but also because I believe that the concept of belief-value matrices will provide a schema which will prove helpful to the other social sciences. I would suggest, in short, that such concepts as "attitude," "culture pattern," "need-disposition," etc., as used by various social scientists, will all be translatable into, and be illuminated by, the concept of belief-value matrices.

In conclusion it would seem meet to indicate the main sources from which I think my ideas have come. First of all most of the credit, if it be credit, should go to all the students whose ideas I have shamefully and consistently adopted and exploited throughout the years, and ended up by believing to be my own. Secondly, it should go to my teachers at Harvard who taught me to think, to be critical, to be complicated but to remain naturalistic. Thirdly, it should go to all the members of the department of psychology at Berkeley who have always given me untold moral and intellectual support in spite of considerable tolerant skepticism as to the worth of my final outpourings. Next, it should go to the Gestalt psychologists, but especially to Kurt Lewin whose ideas I have borrowed time and again and absorbed into my very blood. Again, it should go to my year's stay in Vienna and especially to Egon Brunswik, who opened my eyes to the meaning and the viability of the European psychological tradition, both academic and psychoanalytical, and who gave me new insight into the essentially "achievement" character of behavior. Still further, it should go to all my colleagues, old and young, in the Assessment Program of the Office of Strategic Services. There once and for all I finally became addicted to PSYCHOLOGY and no longer content to think merely of rats and of learning. I there acquired an aspiration level relative to personality psychology which I have since been striving for but have, of course, not achieved. And finally, my thanks must go to the Department of Social Relations at Harvard University, which during the year 1949–50 taught me something of sociology and of anthropology and of personality and of social psychology, and set me wondering about ways in which my rat concepts might eventually become amalgamated with those of the scientists in these other fields. For, if we are to advance, we must first understand, and then attempt to incorporate into our own, the perspectives of our sister sciences—not merely of those sciences which pertain to physiology but also and even more of those which pertain to social living.

7

GENERAL ISSUES IN PSYCHOLOGICAL SCIENCE

The foregoing excerpts from the autobiography of Edward Tolman give a lively picture of the way in which one mind contends first with the sweep and scope of psychology, then eventually finds that approach to the area that it considers both the most productive and the most compatible. By no means do all psychologists, however, care to travel the road that Tolman found a happy one. In psychology, probably more than in other scientific disciplines, there is uncertainty, disagreement, dialogue, and debate about such matters as the most productive general approaches to problems, the most defensible philosophical positions on key issues, and the most nutritious problems for scientific investigation.

While there are no longer any "schools of psychology," in which great men gather around themselves a group of disciples who share certain deep convictions about approaches and procedures, not all psychologists necessarily agree on basic matters of philosophy of science, nor even on central methodological issues. The following two selections, the first by Gordon W. Allport and the second by Robert R. Holt, present several facets of one persisting and lively controversy. Although Robert Holt was not responding directly to Professor Allport's paper, he very clearly is responding to Allport's well-known position concerning individuality and the proper ways to study it.

While both writers show a commitment to the study of personality —a commitment by no means shared by all psychologists—they differ vigorously in their views of the most productive modes of thought and the most realizable aspirations for the field of personality. Are these two approaches inevitably irreconcilable? If so, which is more likely to advance the scientific knowledge of personality?

THE GENERAL AND THE UNIQUE IN PSYCHOLOGICAL SCIENCE*

Gordon W. Allport

Let me take my text from the opening sentence of *Ethical Standards of Psychologists,* the official code set forth by the American Psychological Association (1959). This sentence defines a psychologist as a person "committed to increasing man's understanding of man." The code itself makes it abundantly clear that both *man in general* and *man in particular* are the objects of our concern. Thus the psychologist, as psychologist, can properly make two sorts of statements; he can say:

(1) the problem of human personality concerns me deeply;
(2) the problem of Bill's personality concerns me deeply.

Although superficially similar the two statements are poles apart. In the second we are speaking of one and only one person; in the first we are abstracting elusive properties from all of the three billion inhabitants of the earth. Both statements are true; both appropriate; and both fall squarely within the domain of psychological science.

Some people, to be sure, object to this broad coverage. Artists, literati, some psychiatrists, perhaps a few clinical psychologists, would say that to generalize about personality is to lose it. Bill, as an integral datum, we are told, cannot belong to scientific psychology. He can be represented only by the methods of biography, drama, or other artistic portraiture. Bill himself might say to the psychologists, "If you think those pockmarks on your silly IBM card represent *me,* you have another guess coming."

It does no good to argue that every individual system in nature is unique; every rat, every porpoise, every worm; and that it is only the general laws of their functioning that lead to comprehension. No, we can't take this easy way out of the dilemma. The human system, unlike all others, possesses a degree of openness to the world, a degree of foresight and self-awareness, a flexibility and binding of functions and goals that present a unique structural challenge far more insistent than that presented by any other living system. It is because of their essential stereotypy and lack of variation that psychologists like to

* Abridged from *Journal of Personality,* Vol. 30, 1962, pp. 405–422. By permission.

draw their generalizations from lower animals. But for my part I venture the opinion that all of the infrahuman vertebrates in the world differ less from one another in psychological functioning and in complexity of organization, than one human being does from any other.

And so I wonder whether the time has not come for students of personality to shake themselves loose from a too-rigid response set, and perhaps even to reverse it. Instead of growing impatient with the single case and hastening on to generalization, why should we not grow impatient with our generalizations and hasten to the internal pattern? For one thing we should ask, are our generalizations really relevant to the case we are studying? If so, do they need modification? And in what ways is this individual the asymptote of all our general laws?

Or to state the procedure more simply: Why should we not start with individual behavior as a source of hunches (as we have in the past), and then seek our generalizations (also as we have in the past), but finally come back to the individual—not for the mechanical application of laws (as we do now), but for a fuller, supplementary, and more accurate assessment than we are now able to give? I suspect that the reason our present assessments are now so often feeble and sometimes even ridiculous, is because we do not take this final step. We stop with our wobbly laws of personality and seldom confront them with the concrete person.

The Dimensional and the Morphogenic

The issue before us is not new. More than a hundred years ago John Stuart Mill proposed that we distinguish sharply between psychology, the science of mind-in-general, and ethology, a science of character (having no relation to what is called ethology today). To his mind ethology should trace the operation of psychological laws in specifically individual combinations—such as the pattern of the single person or of a single culture or nation. Somewhat similar was Dilthey's proposal to distinguish between "explanatory" and "understanding" psychology. Said Dilthey, "We explain nature, but we understand human beings." Windelband too would recognize two classes of science: the nomothetic (seeking general laws) and the idiographic (dealing with structured pattern).

In confronting this same problem William James almost threw up his hands in despair. It is well known that after writing his textbook, he concluded that general psychological laws are poor stuff. He declared that psychology has not produced "a single law in the sense in which physics shows us laws. . . . This is no science, it is only the hope of a science" (1961 ed., p. 335). Perhaps the ensuing half-century of intensive research would have strengthened his faith in general laws; but I doubt it. At any rate he not only questioned the validity of general laws but, champion of the individual though he was, he seemed to feel that the concrete person must also inevitably elude psychology. In his *Memories and Studies* (1912) he wrote,

> . . . in every concrete individual, there is a uniqueness that defies all formulation. We can feel the touch of it and recognize its taste, so to speak, relishing or disliking, as the case may be, but we can give no ultimate account of it, and have in the end simply to admire the Creator (pp. 109 f.).

And so at the end of his career James seems to despair of psychology as a science of either the general or the concrete.

It would serve no good purpose here to review the long-standing debate between partisans of the nomothetic and idiographic methods, between champions of explanation and understanding. Indeed, to insure more rapid progress I think it best to avoid traditional terms altogether. For the purposes of our present discussion I shall speak of "dimensional" and "morphogenic" procedures. Let me explain the latter term.

The science of molecular biology shows us that life-substances are identical across species. The building blocks of life—vegetable and animal—turn out to be strikingly uniform in terms of nucleic acids, protein molecules, and enzymatic reactions. Yet an antelope differs from an ash tree, a man from an antelope, and one man is very unlike another. The challenge of morphogenesis (accounting for pattern) grows more rather than less acute as we discover the commonalities of life. Yet biologists admit that morphogenic biology lags far behind molecular (or dimensional) biology. So too does morphogenic psychology lag far behind dimensional psychology.

The commonalities in personality are the horizontal dimensions that run through all individuals. We focus our attention chiefly upon these commonalities: for example, upon the common traits of achievement, anxiety, extraversion, dominance, creativity; or upon the common processes of learning, repression, identification, aging. We spend scarcely one per cent of our research time discovering whether these common dimensions are in reality relevant to Bill's personality, and if so, how they are patterned together to compose the Billian quality of Bill. Ideally, research should explore both horizontal and vertical dimensions.

I have already rejected the easy solution that assigns the general to science and the unique to art. I should like also to dispose of another proposed solution. Some psychologists would say that Bill, our individual, is known primarily by his conformity to, or deviation from, universal norms or group norms. His private and unique qualities are only the residual peculiarities left over when we have accounted for most of his behavior in terms of general norms. My colleagues, Professors Kluckhohn, Murray, and Schneider (1953, p. 53) have expressed the thought by saying every man is in certain respects:

a. like all other men (universal norms)
b. like some other men (group norms)
c. like no other man (idosyncratic norms)

Now it is certainly true that we often wish to use universal and group norms. We want to know whether Bill, relative to others, is high or low in intelligence, in dominance, in affiliativeness. But although Bill can be compared profitably on many dimensions with the average human being or with his cultural group, still he himself weaves all these attributes into a unique idiomatic system. His personality does not contain three systems, but only one. Whatever individuality is, it is not the residual ragbag left over after general dimensions have been exhausted. The organization of Bill's life is first, last, and all the time, the primary fact of his human nature.

Since we cannot brush our problem aside we do well to ask how a truly morphogenic psychology (sadly neglected up to now) can become a scientific asset. To become such it will have to learn certain lessons from dimensional empiricism, and from positivism—most of all the lesson of observer reliability. It is not sufficient to "intuit" the pattern of Bill or Betty. All of their friends do this much, with greater or less success. A science, even a morphogenic science, should be made of sterner stuff. The morphogenic interpretations we make should be testable, communicable, and have a high measure of predictive power.

My purpose is to suggest certain procedures that seem to me to be morphogenic in nature, or at least semi-morphogenic, and yet to be at the same time controlled, repeatable, reliable. Before I do so, let us look more closely at the question of successful prediction, which, we are told, is the acid test of a valid science.

Prediction: Dimensional and Morphogenic

Prediction based on general or dimensional information is called actuarial. For many purposes it is surprisingly accurate. One marvels, for example, at the correctness with which insurance companies predict the number of deaths that will occur by highway accidents, from cancer, or from suicide. The chances of a hypothetical average man for survival or death are all the insurance business wants to know. Whether Bill himself will be one of the fatal cases it cannot tell—and that is what Bill wants to know.

The situation is exactly the same in psychology. Actuarial prediction enables us, with fair success, to predict what proportion of boys, having a certain type of physique and family history, will become delinquent; what percentage of engaged couples, having various types of background, will enjoy successful marriage. Actuarial prediction can tell approximately what the average student's university record will be on the basis of his elementary school record or I.Q. It can advise industry concerning crucial cutting points on psychological tests by designating the score below which most applicants would probably fail on the job.

Suppose we take John, a lad of 12 years, and suppose his family background is poor; his father was a criminal; his mother rejected him; his neighborhood is marginal. Suppose that 70 per cent of the boys having a similar background become criminals. Does this mean that John himself has a 70 per cent chance of delinquency? Not at all. John is a unique being, with a genetic inheritance all his own; his life-experience is his own. His unique world contains influences unknown to the statistician: perhaps an affectionate relation with a certain teacher, or a wise word once spoken by a neighbor. Such factors may be decisive and may offset all average probabilities. There is no 70 per cent chance about John. He either will or will not become delinquent. Only a complete understanding of his personality, of his present and future circumstances, will give us a basis for such prediction.

It was this line of argument, I believe, that led Meehl (1954) to say, "Let us see what the research evidence is regarding the relative success of dimensional and morphogenic prediction." Surveying such relevant studies as were available, Meehl concludes that morphogenic (what he calls "clinical") prediction seems to be actually inferior. More successful are predictions made mechanically with the aid of a standard formula. Best to keep strictly to our Rorschach diagnostic signs, to our I.Q. measures, to our profile on the Minnesota Multiphasic Personality Inventory, and to other standard predictive indexes. We can, of course, weight the signs, but we must do so according to rule. We may give one sign twice as much weight as another, just as a cook uses two cups of flour but only one of sugar. Meehl appropriately calls the procedure he advocates the "cookbook" method.

The point is that whenever we deal with well-defined variables, possessing a known relation to a pathological type, or to success in occupation or in school, we are usually safer in following the cookbook method of combining scores according to a formula known to have a good average validity. If strictly followed the logical outcome of this procedure would be the early elimination of the clinician or practitioner as assessor or diagnostician. A computing machine could handle the data more accurately than a fallible psychologist. In coming years we shall, no doubt, increasingly encounter IBM diagnoses and IBM predictions in psychological practice. It does no good to shudder at such a *lèse majesté* to human dignity. It will surely come to pass. But already we can sense its limitations.

Limitations of the Cookbook

In the first place, as Meehl (1957) himself has pointed out, the cookbook is usable only under restricted circumstances. The dimensions studied must be objectively defined, reliably measured, validly related to the target of prediction (e.g., to vocational success), clearly normed for a population to which the subject belongs. Most of the dimensions we employ have not attained this level of objective perfection.

Again, by keeping within a previously established dimensional frame the cookbook procedure rules out insights peculiarly relevant to the individual. True, the computer can tell whether Sam should be diagnosed as schizophrenic. But whether Sam's love for his sister and her way of dealing with him are such as to effect his recovery, the computer cannot tell. A dimensional frame is a rigid thing. It is like giving to the cook ingredients that will produce only dumplings while imagining that she has the freedom to produce a cake.

Further, the dimensions imposed on the individual are dimensions of interest to the investigator, or to the hospital, school, or firm. For this reason they may not be relevant in guiding John. The most salient features of his life—his aspirations, his sense of duty, his existential pattern, may be left untouched. In every dimensional analysis there are inevitably many "empty cells."

Finally, as for the discovery that clinical or morphogenic predictions are in fact poorer than cookbook predictions, I can only say, "What a pitiful reflection on the inventiveness and sensitivity of psychologists!" The findings—which, by the way, are not necessarily the last word on the matter—prove only that we do not yet know how to maximize clinical skill through training. I suspect that our present emphasis on tests and cookbooks may actually be damaging the potential skill of young clinicians and advisers. There are studies that indicate that clinicians grow confused when they have too many data concerning an individual life, and that for this reason their predictions are better when they fall back on a mere formula (Sarbin, Taft, and Bailey, 1960, pp. 262–264). But this finding, too, points chiefly to our neglect in inventing and training in sensitive morphogenic methods.

Recently, Meehl (1959) has shown that under certain circumstances a combined actuarial and clinical—a kind of "configural"—procedure is superior in predictive power to either method used alone. This is progress indeed. But I would raise two objections: (1) the level of success achieved is still too low; (2) the diagnostic instruments employed in the first instance are too one-sided. The original instruments on which the predictions are based are nearly always of a dimensional or horizontal order (extending across people) and seldom of an intensive vertical order (within the person).

My point is that while dimensional diagnostic methods are an indispensable half of the psychologist's tools of trade, the other half of the tool box is, up to now, virtually empty. I recall that a few years before his death I was discussing this matter with the beloved psychologist Edward Tolman. He said to me with his characteristic twinkle, employing the then-current terminology, "I know I should be more idiographic in my research, but I just don't know how to be." My reply now, as then, is, "Let's learn!"

Morphogenic Methods

To start simply: it is worth asking whether we ought to seek only objective validation for our measuring instruments. Why not demand likewise, where possible, subjective validation by asking our subject what he himself thinks of the dimensional diagnosis we have made? (If the subject is a child, a psychotic, or manifestly defensive, this step, of course, has no point.) Too often we fail to consult the richest of all sources of data, namely, the subject's own self-knowledge. During the war psychiatrists were assigned the task of screening candidates for the armed services. While they employed various dimensional tests, it is said that the best predictive question turned out to be, "Do you feel that you are emotionally ready to enter military service?" The men themselves were often the best judges—although, of course, not infallible.

It is true that psychiatrists and clinical psychologists have long known that they should take the patient's own story as a starting point. But almost immediately they redact this story into general categories, dismembering the complex pattern of the life into standard dimensions (abilities, needs, interest inventories, and the like), and hasten to assign scores on their favorite variables. One notes too that therapists who claim to be existential in their orientation also tend to employ standard procedures in treatment. Their techniques and even their interpretations are sometimes indistinguishable from orthodox psychoanalysis (G. W. Allport, 1961a).

But let us turn now to what at present lies available in the morphogenic half of our tool box. My inventory will be illustrative rather than exhaustive. I shall be brief in describing each method, hoping that the array as a whole will help to make clear what I mean by morphogenic method, and, best of all, may stimulate further invention.

1. Familiar is the method of matching, used with profit by both German and American investigators (see G. W. Allport, 1961b, pp. 387 f. and 446 f.). This method invites us to fit together any record of personal expression, however complex, with any other record. We test our skill in seeing that this case record must fit such-and-such a test profile; or that this handwriting goes with that voice. It is a good way to discover how much of a perceptible form-quality saturates separate performances. Although the method gives us no insight into causal relationships it is, so far as it goes, a good example of a 100 per cent morphogenic procedure.

2. Another wholly morphogenic technique was devised by Baldwin (1942) who made use of a long series of personal letters written by one woman, Jenny by name. Her unique thought-structure, i.e., associative complexes, was the object of interest. If she talked about women, money, or nature, with what feeling-tone did she mention them? If she mentioned her son what else did she mention in the same context? This technique, called by Baldwin "personal structure analy-

sis," is highly revealing, and is carried through without reference to any general or dimensional norms.

3. Somewhat similar, and wholly morphogenic, is the procedure recommended by Shapiro (1961) for psychiatrists. On the basis of a five-hour intensive interview with a patient he constructs a questionnaire which from that time on is standard for this patient but not directly relevant to any other patient. Administered over intervals of months or years, the instrument will show the course of development, including improvement or deterioration in health.

4. A somewhat more ambitious attempt, still wholly morphogenic, would be to attempt to discover the number and range of all the major structural foci a given life possesses. Many years ago in his *Experiment in Autobiography,* H. G. Wells asserted that there were only two major themes in his life: interest in world government and in sex. Elsewhere I have explored the possibility that a life may be understood almost completely by tracing only a few major themes or intentions. Probably two is too few for most lives (perhaps especially for H. G. Wells), although it is said that Tolstoy after his conversion had only one major theme: viz., the simplification of life. More typical, I believe, would be the case of William James, who, according to his biographer, R. B. Perry [in *The Thought and Character of William James,* 1935, chaps. 90–91], had eight dominant trends. In some preliminary explorations with my students (G. W. Allport, 1958), I find that they regard it possible to characterize a friend adequately on the average with 7.2 essential characteristics, the range falling for the most part between 3 and 10.

What to call these central motifs I do not exactly know. They are "essential characteristics," for the most part motivational in type although some seem to be stylistic. F. H. Allport (1937) has proposed the term "teleonomic trends" and suggests that we proceed to regard them as life-hypotheses held by the individual, and count carefully how many of his daily acts can accurately be ordered to one or more of these trends. The idea has merit but it has not yet been systematically tried out. One question is whether we can obtain sufficiently high observer-reliability (i.e., reliable judgments of the fit of specific acts to the hypothesized trend). At present it is only one of the avenues of research needing exploration.

5. Suppose we are interested in an individual's value system. Direct questioning is useful, of course. "What would you rather have than anything else in the world?" "What experiences give you a feeling of completeness, of fully functioning, or of personal identity?"

"What," in Maslow's terms, "are your peak experiences of life?" Elsewhere I have argued strongly for the use of such direct questions as these, for in important matters we should grant our client the right to be believed. Projective methods should never be used without direct methods, for we cannot interpret the results of projective testing unless we know whether they confirm or contradict the subject's own self-image (see G. W. Allport, 1960, chap. 6).

But how can we grow more precise in this type of work, benefitting from lessons learned from objective dimensional procedures? One such technique is the "self-anchoring scale," devised by Kilpatrick and Cantril (1960). It consists of a simple diagram of a ladder, having 10 rungs. The subject is asked first to describe in his own terms the "very best or ideal way of life" that he can imagine. Then he is told that rung 10 at the top of the ladder represents this ideal. Similarly he is asked to describe the "worst possible way of life" for himself. This he is told is the bottom of the ladder. Now he is asked to point to the rung on the ladder where he thinks he stands today—somewhere between the bottom and top rungs. He can also be asked, "Where on this scale were you two years ago? Five years ago? Where do you think you will be five years hence?"

This device has considerable value in personal counseling. It is also used by the authors to study rising or falling morale in different countries, e.g., in those having undergone recent revolution as compared with those living in a static condition. In this case, a curious thing happens, a completely morphogenic instrument is adapted for use as a tool for nomothetic research. Ordinarily, of course, the situation is reversed: it is a nomothetic mold that is forced upon the individual.

All these various examples suffice to show that it is possible to examine the internal and unique pattern of personal structure without any dependence whatsoever on universal or group norms. All the methods I have mentioned up to now are completely morphogenic, although they are seldom explicitly recognized as such.

Semi-Morphogenic Methods

Let us turn our attention to certain procedures that are highly useful for exploring individuality even though they are in part also dimensional.

6. First, there is the common dimensional instrument, the rating scale. Many years ago Conrad (1932) asked teachers to rate pupils

on 231 common traits. The teachers were thus forced to make the assumption that all children did in fact possess all 231 traits in some degree. Proceeding on this assumption the teachers agreed poorly, as reflected in a median reliability coefficient of .48. After this nomothetic orgy, the same teachers were asked to star only those traits that they considered to be "central or dominating importance in the child's personality." On this part of their task the teachers agreed almost perfectly, their judgments correlating .95. This result shows that low reliability may be due to the essential irrelevance of many of the dimensions we forcibly apply to an individual. On well-configurated prominent dispositions there is likely to be good agreement.

7. Another half-way method is the Role Construct Repertory Test, devised by Kelly (1955). The method asks the subject to tell in what way two concepts are alike and how they differ from a third. The concepts might, for example, be *mother, sister, wife*. The subject could, for instance, reply that mother and sister are alike because both are comforting, and the wife different because she is demanding. Not only is the particular response revealing of his family attitudes, but over a long series of comparisons it may turn out that the subject has a characteristic cognitive style in which the polarity of comfortableness vs. demandingness may recur time and time again. This method is not wholly morphogenic since it prescribes for the subject what "significant others" he shall characterize, and in other ways limits his spontaneous choices, but it allows none the less for a certain amount of morphogenic discovery.

8. Certain other devices for approaching cognitive style likewise move in a desirable direction. I have in mind Broverman (1960) who employs standard tests with his subjects, but makes his interpretations entirely in terms of the subject's tendency to do well or poorly on a given type of test relative to his own mean for all tests. By the use of such ipsative scores he is able to determine which responses are strong or weak with respect to other responses within the same individual.

9. Another mixed method is the Allport-Vernon-Lindzey *Study of Values* (1960), devised to measure the relative prominence of each of the six Spranger *Lebensformen* within a particular person. The resulting profile does not tell how high or low a given person stands on the economic, theoretic, or religious value in the population at large, but only which value is relatively most, or next most, or least prominent in his own life. This type of profile is semi-dimensional, semi-morphogenic.

10. Sometimes the *Q* sort (Stephenson, 1953) is said to be an idiographic technique. Yet it, like other devices we are now considering, goes only part way. It has the merit of making use of self-report, and can be used for measuring changes in the self concept. As ordinarily used, however, only a standard set of propositions is employed, thus creating for the subject little more than a standard rating scale. And if the subject is forced, as he often is, to produce a quasi-normal distribution among his sorts he is further restricted. In short, the method can be rigidly dimensional. Yet it is a flexible method, and some variants are highly promising, perhaps especially when combined with inverse factor analysis.

11. For example, Nunnally (1955) studied one therapy case over a two-year period, using 60 statements selected for their unique relevance to this person (and this, I think, is a great improvement over the use of uniform lists). The patient made her sorts under many different sets of instructions on many occasions. Using an inverse factor analysis it was possible to find three fairly independent factors that comprised her total self concept. During therapy these factors showed only a moderate change.

It strikes me as curious that out of the thousands and thousands of factor-analytic studies that smother us today, scarcely any are carried through in such a manner as to discover the internal, unique, organizational units that characterize a single life. Even inverse factor analysis does not fully achieve this goal unless the initial information employed is selected for its morphogenic relevance. A good deal of creative work still lies ahead for factor analysis. It has potentiality, I think, for discovering the main foci of organization in a given life, but has not yet moved far enough in this direction.

Final Word

This survey of possible relevant methods is not complete, but may indicate that by a deliberate shift of procedures we can bring the laggard end of our science up to a more flourishing level. To effect the shift we shall have to restrain to some extent our present dimensional debauch.

In this paper I have introduced the term "morphogenic psychology," borrowed from, but not identical with the usage in, biology. It is, I think, a good term, better than "idiographic" which so many students of personality misuse and misspell. I hope the concept "morphogenic" catches on, but even more do I hope that the types of research to which I have ventured to apply the label will flourish and spread. Already we know that personality (in general) is an interesting topic for study. But only when morphogenic methods are more highly developed shall we be able to do justice to the fascinating individuality that marks the personalities of Bill, John, and Betty.

REFERENCES

Allport, F. H. Teleonomic description in the study of personality. *Char. & Pers.*, 1937, **6**, 202–214.

Allport, G. W. What units shall we employ? Chap. 9 in G. Lindzey (Ed.), *Assessment of human motives.* New York: Rinehart, 1958. Also chap. 7 in G. W. Allport, *Personality and social encounter.* Boston: Beacon, 1960.

Allport, G. W. The trend in motivational theory. Chap. 6 in *Personality and social encounter.* Boston: Beacon, 1960.

Allport, G. W., Vernon, P. E., and Lindzey, G. *A study of values.* (3rd ed.) Boston: Houghton Mifflin, 1960.

Allport, G. W. Comment. In R. May (Ed.), *Existential psychology.* New York: Random House, 1961. Pp. 94–99. (a)

Allport, G. W. *Pattern and growth in personality.* New York: Holt, Rinehart & Winston, 1961. (b)

American Psychological Association. Ethical standards of psychologists. *Amer. Psychologist,* 1959, **14**, 279–282.

Baldwin, A. L. Personal structure analysis: A statistical method for investigation of the single personality. *J. abnorm. soc. Psychol.,* 1942, **37**, 163–183.

Broverman, D. M. Cognitive style and intra-individual variation in abilities. *J. Pers.,* 1960, **28**, 240–256.

Conrad, H. S. The validity of personality ratings of preschool children. *J. educ. Psychol.,* 1932, **23**, 671–680.

James, W. *Memories and studies.* New York: Longmans, Green, 1912.

James, W. *Psychology: The briefer course.* G. W. Allport (Ed.). New York: Harper, Torchbooks, 1961.

Kelly, G. A. *The psychology of personal constructs.* Vol. 1. New York: Norton, 1955.

Kilpatrick, F. P., and Cantril, H. Self-anchoring scale: A measure of the individual's unique reality world. *J. indiv. Psychol.,* 1960, **16**, 158–170.

Kluckhohn, C. M., Murray, H. A., and Schneider, D. M. (Eds.). *Personality in nature, society, and culture.* New York: Knopf, 1953.

Meehl, P. E. *Clinical vs. statistical prediction.* Minneapolis: Univ. of Minnesota Press, 1954.

Meehl, P. E. When shall we use our heads instead of a formula? *J. counsel. Psychol.*, 1957, **4**, 268–273.

Meehl, P. E. A comparison of clinicians with five statistical methods of identifying psychotic MMPI profiles. *J. counsel. Psychol.*, 1959, **6**, 102–109.

Nunnally, J. C. An investigation of some propositions of self-conception: The case of Miss Sun. *J. abnorm soc. Psychol.*, 1955, **50**, 87–92.

Sarbin, T. R., Taft, R., and Bailey, D. E. *Clinical inference and cognitive theory*. New York: Holt, Rinehart & Winston, 1960.

Shapiro, M. B. The single case in fundamental clinical psychological research. *Brit. J. med. Psychol.*, 1961, **34**, 255–262.

Stephenson, W. *The study of behavior*. Chicago: Univ. of Chicago Press, 1953.

INDIVIDUALITY AND GENERALIZATION IN THE PSYCHOLOGY OF PERSONALITY*

Robert R. Holt

One of the hardiest perennial weeds in psychology's conceptual garden is the notion that there are nomothetic (generalizing) and idiographic (individualizing) branches, types, or emphases of science. Many respected and important contributors to psychology—especially to personology, the psychology of personality—have quoted these terms with respect and have used them as if they contributed something useful to methodology (cf. Allport, 1937; Beck, 1953; Bellak, 1956; Bertalanffy, 1951; Colby, 1958; Dymond, 1953; Falk, 1956; Hoffman, 1960; Sarbin, 1944; Stephenson, 1953; the list could be considerably extended).

The principal exponent of the nomothetic-idiographic dichotomy in this country has been Gordon W. Allport (1937, 1940, 1942, 1946, 1955), a pioneer in academic personology and a man who has brilliantly clarified many important issues in the field. On this particular point, I shall try to show, the artist in him has probably dimmed the vision of the scientist. The underlying problem with which Allport

* Abridged from *Journal of Personality*, Vol. 30, 1962, pp. 377–404. By permission.

wrestles is vexing enough: the unusual nature of personality as a scientific subject matter. Allport readily concedes that everything in nature is unique, but maintains that natural sciences are not interested in the unique leaf, stone, or river. Only personology, the argument continues, takes as its very subject matter the unique personality as opposed to the generalized human mind or the behavior of organisms at large. The rest of psychology takes care of the general laws of behavior and experience and is thus nomothetic (literally, setting down laws); what is left over is the impressive fact that every personality is different, and must be studied in such ways as respect and try to capture this uniqueness—in short, by an idiographic science (literally, portraying what is private or peculiar; i.e., individual). With these two curious words adopted from Windelband, then, Allport describes what he sees as two complementary branches of psychology, both of which are necessary for complete coverage.

On the other hand, many distinguished contributors to personology, from Freud to Murphy (1947), have found no need for such an approach to the scientific study of individuality, and the sharp voice of Eysenck (1954) has been heard rebutting Beck (1953) and proclaiming that psychology should be nomothetic throughout. Clearly, the issue is controversial.

The Historical Role of Differential Psychology

In psychology, the romantic movement has been felt particularly in personology, the psychology of personality. And one reason that its impact was particularly great there is the fact that personology grew out of differential psychology, the psychology of individual differences.

The first efforts of the "new psychology" of the 1890's were devoted to finding empirical generalizations and abstract laws about such functions as sensation and perception (concepts which themselves were the heritage of faculty psychology). It was what Boring has called the science of the average, healthy adult (and, one might add, male) mind, a subtly Aristotelian conception that relegated the study of women and children, and of abnormal and exceptional behavior generally, to a subordinate status. Even so, there remained embarrassing observations of exceptions to the general laws even when the subjects were "average, healthy adults"; and so the field of differential psychology was invented as a kind of wastebasket to take care of these annoying anomalies. From the standpoint of the highest type of psychology, which was concerned with laws in a way not expected of differential psychology, the unexplained residual variance continued to be considered error and to be treated as if it were random and unlawful.

The psychologists who were content to work with the miscellany of leavings from all the high-caste tables in psychology were further handicapped by the taint of practical application, for they were principally involved in applying psychology to mundane problems like educating children, treating the disturbed, and selecting employees. Such work called for the prediction of behavior, and it quickly became apparent that the general laws provided by "scientific psychology" left a great deal unpredicted; it was practically imperative to supplement them by some kind of lore that dealt with all the other important determinants.

As time went on, differential psychologists made a radical shift in approach. In the era when individual differences were thought of as error—as not lawful, really—they were catalogued and measured, and a few attempts were made to parcel out the variance in terms of sex, age, ethnic group, and other gross demographic categories. During the past couple of decades, however, personologists have increasingly begun to recognize that all the error-terms of standard psychological equations are their own happy hunting grounds. Individual differences in such hallowed perceptual phenomena as time-error, size-estimation, and shape-constancy proved to be not random at all but reliably related to other dimensions of individual differences in cognitive phenomena and in noncognitive realms, too (cf. Gardner, Holzman, Klein, Linton, and Spence, 1959).

The fallacy involved in treating individual differences as if they were random and unlawful resembles that of the nineteenth-century scientists who concretized Newton's laws as propositions concerning mechanical bodies. In both cases, the grasp of certain principles lagged behind what could have been expected. Objectively viewed, the laws that govern individual variation in the perception of apparent movement are just as abstract as the laws that cover the general case, and seem to have a different methodological status only because of the accident of history that brought about the discovery of the latter first. And, despite the implied promise in Klein and Schlesinger's title (1949), the study of such general principles does not bring the perceiver, the person in Stern's sense, back into perceptual psychology; it is merely a change in the axis of generalization, so to speak, not a way of becoming less abstract about perception.

The Logic of the Romantic Point of View in Personology

Let us now consider each of the main propositions that make up the romantic point of view, and state the logical objections to them systematically.

1. *The goal of personology must be understanding, not prediction and control.* The goal of those who profess an idiographic point of view is not anything so antiseptic and inhuman as a family of curves; it is *understanding*. In one sense, it is proper to say that we understand poliomyelitis when we have isolated the responsible viruses and have identified the conditions under which they attack and cripple a person, but this is not *Verstehen*. That conception is an empathic, intuitive *feeling* of knowing a phenomenon from the inside, as it were. To take a more congenial example, we do not understand why a particular boy becomes delinquent from knowing that he comes from a neighborhood that an ecological survey has determined to be economically deprived and socially disorganized; whereas after we have read Farrell's *Studs Lonigan* and have seen such conditions and the embeddedness of delinquency in them portrayed with artistic power and vividness, then we understand (in the sense of *Verstehen*) the relation between these phenomena.

From this example, it should be clear that the feeling of understanding is a subjective effect aimed at by artists, not scientists. In science, when we say we understand something, we mean that we can predict and control it, but such aims are foreign to the romantic viewpoint. When Allport says (as of course Freud and many others have said also) that novelists and poets have been great intuitive psychologists, in some ways the greatest psychologists, the statement has two (not necessarily coexistent) meanings: that literary men have known many significant variables of and propositions about personality (e.g., the role of unconscious incestuous wishes in determining many kinds of behavior), or, that they have been able to create the most vivid, compelling portraits of people, which give us the sense of knowing and understanding them. The latter effect is achieved by judicious selection and artful distortion, not by exhaustive cataloguing and measurement of traits, motives, or structural relations. Indeed, the idea of a catalogue is the very antithesis of art, just as a painful realism that tries to copy nature slavishly is the death of an artistic endeavor.

Here we see the issues drawn clearly. Is personology to be an art, devoted to word portraits that seek to evoke in the reader the thrill of recognition, the gratifying (if perhaps illusory) feeling of understanding unique individuals? Or is it to be a science, which enables us to study these same persons in all their uniqueness and to derive from such study general propositions about the structure, development, and other significant aspects of personality? If we elect for a science, we must abandon art whenever it takes us in a different direction than the one demanded by the scientific method, and we must recognize that the ideal of an idiographic science is a will-o'-the-wisp, an artistic and not a scientific goal. Science may be supplemented by art, but not combined with it.

2. *The proper methods of personology are intuition and empathy, which have no place in natural science.* As has been indicated above, intuition and empathy were used by the romantics as ways of gaining direct and definitive understanding, and were considered to be complete scientific methods. The contemporary personologist has no quarrel with their use in the practical arts of clinical psychology and psychoanalysis, nor as ways of making discoveries and formulating hypotheses. Indeed, the more secure scientists are in the methodological position, the more respect they usually have for intuition (and in psychology for the closely related methods of empathy and recipathy). Thus, the claim that these operations have no place in natural science is false; they are used by all scientists in the most exciting and creative phase of scientific work: when they decide what to study, what variables to control, what empirical strategies to use, and when they make discoveries within the structure of empirical data. As to their sufficiency, I need only remind the reader that the methodology of verification, the hypothesis-testing phase of scientific work, involves well-developed rules and consensually established procedures, and that intuition and empathy have no place in it.

3. *Personology is a subjective discipline as contrasted to objective branches of psychology, being concerned with values and meanings, which cannot be subjected to quantification.* Elsewhere (Holt, 1961), I have dealt with the contention that there is a fundamental methodological difference between disciplines that deal with verbal meanings and values, and those that deal with objective facts. Briefly, the argument is the familiar one that objectivity is only intersubjectivity, and that meanings (including values) may be perceived and dealt with in essentially the same ways as the data of natural science, which must be discriminated and recognized also. Moreover, a logical analysis of the operations carried out in disciplines such as literature, concerned with the understanding of individual works and little (if at all)

with generalization, shows that these workers outside of science use many of the *same* methods of analyzing texts as the quantitative content-analysts of social psychology, with their exclusive concern with generalization. Their work has shown that meanings may be quantified and in other ways treated as objectively as any other facts of nature. Other objections to quantification grow out of antipathy to abstract variables of analysis, and will be considered in the following section.

4. *The concepts of personology must be individualized, not generalized as are the concepts of natural science.* The belief that the concern of personology with unique individuals (see below) contrasts fundamentally with the exclusive concern of nomothetic science with generalities logically implies that the two types of discipline must have different types of concepts. As the chief spokesman for the romantic point of view in psychology, Allport calls for the use of individual traits, which are specific to the person being studied, not common traits, which are assumed to be present to some degree in all persons. But to describe an individual trait, we have to take one of two courses: either we create a unique word (a neologism) for each unique trait, or we use a unique configuration of existing words. The first approach is clearly impossible for communication, let alone science; personology would be a complete Babel. The second solution, however, turns out to be a concealed form of nomothesis, for what is a unique configuration of existing words but a "fallacious attempt to capture something ineffably individual by a complex net of general concepts"? Allport himself has explicitly ruled out this possibility:

> . . . each psychologist tends to think of individuals as combinations of whatever abstractions he favors for psychological analysis. This procedure, common as it is, is wholly unsuitable for the psychology of personality. For one thing, such abstract units are not distinctively *personal.* (1937, p. 239)

An idiographic discipline thus must be a dumb or an incomprehensible one, for intelligible words—even some of Allport's favorite, literary ones, like *Falstaffian,* which he does consider "personal"—abstract and generalize, proclaiming a general pattern of resemblance between at least two unique individuals, Falstaff and the case being described. Any such trait thus becomes common, not individual.

One of the great methodologists of social science, Max Weber (1949) developed an apposite analysis of scientific concepts and their development in reaction against the romantic movement in his country at the turn of the century (cf. Parsons, 1957). He had the insight to see that the exponents of *Geisteswissenschaft* were trying to do the impossible: to capture the full richness of reality. There are three identifiable stages in the scientific study of anything, Weber said. To begin with, one selects from nature the historical individual (or class thereof) one wishes to focus on; for example, the Boston Massacre, the personality of Einstein, the cathedral at Chartres. Even though limited, each of these is infinitely rich in potentially specifiable aspects and configurations. One could study one of these, or even a tiny "flower in a crannied well," until doomsday and not exhaust everything that could be known about it. Without doing any more abstracting than focusing on a particular topic, one can only contemplate it; and this is where the idiographic approach logically must stop. The method of intuition or *Verstehen* is essentially a wordless act of identification with the object, or some other attempt to "live in it" without analyzing its Gestalt.

The second stage, that of the ideal type, is a rudimentary attempt to see similarities between historical individuals, while staying as close as possible to their concrete particularity. Ideal types are much used in psychology, especially in diagnosis, for any syndrome such as schizophrenia is a complex of identifiably separate but loosely covarying elements, never encountered in exact textbook form. The lure of ideal types is that they give the brief illusion of getting you close to the individual while still allowing a degree of generality. But this advantage is illusory, the apparent advantage of a compromise that denies satisfaction to either party. Concrete reality (fidelity to the unique individual *is* forsworn, and the advantages of truly general concepts are not attained. An ideal type does not fit any particular case exactly, and the failure of fit is different in kind as well as degree from one case to another. For an ideal type "is a conceptual construct which is neither historical reality nor even the 'true' reality. It is even less fitted to serve as a schema under which a real situation or action is to be subsumed as one *instance*. It has the significance of a purely ideal *limiting* concept with which the real situation or action is compared and surveyed for the explication of certain of its significant components." (Weber, 1949, p. 93)

The final stage of scientific development, therefore, is the fractionation of ideal types into their constituent dimensions and elements, which Weber called abstract analytical variables. Paradoxically, only a truly abstract concept can give an exact fit to any particular individual! I cannot say exactly how Falstaffian or how schizophrenic or how big any particular subject may be, but I can name a particular value of an abstract analytical variable, height, that fits him as closely as his skin. The example would be less convincing if chosen from psychology because we do not have as well-established, unitary dimensions as the physical ones, and not as simple and unarguable operations for measuring them as the use of the meter stick; the principle, however, is the same.

5. *The only kind of analysis allowable in personology is structural, not abstract, while natural science is not concerned with structure.* It is true that the scientific psychology of Dilthey's heyday had no place for structural analysis in the sense introduced by the romantics. Psychology dealt with a number of functions, which were treated implicitly or explicitly as quite independent of one another. It had no methods parallel to those of exegetic Biblical scholarship or literary criticism, which seek out the internal organization of ideas in a specific text. And the reductionistic enthusiasts for analyzing things were not interested in putting the pieces back together again, nor very clear themselves that analysis need not mean dismemberment. This state of affairs made it easy to think that analysis could be destructive, and that structural relations between the parts of the personality could be studied only in concrete, unique individuals, so that structure[1] seemed to be an exclusive concern of idiographic disciplines.

There are really two points here: the distrust of analysis, and the emphasis on structure. The first of these has been partly dealt with in the preceding section; it was based on a misunderstanding of the nature of abstract concepts.

On the second point, structural concepts and structural analyses are commonplace in science at large today. Such structural disciplines as stereochemistry and circuit design were (at best) in their infancy at the time of the idiographic manifestoes. Today, natural science uses abstract, structural, and dispositional concepts simultaneously with a minimum of confusion. Presumably, the same may be true of personology someday, too.

At the same time, however, Freud (1947) was developing the

[1] Ironically, in psychology the adherents of structuralism were among those who carried atomistic, reductionistic analysis to its most absurd extreme: the Titchenerian introspectionists. The Gestalt psychologists, though appalled by the equally atomistic behaviorism and structuralism alike, concentrated their efforts on perceptual patterning, leaving untouched most of the structural problems that concern personology, particularly the enduring invariances of molar behavior.

structural point of view in psychoanalysis, and today psychoanalytic psychology is increasingly concerned with the problem and has developed a variety of variables to deal with it (cf. Rapaport and Gill, 1959; Holt, 1960; and see the recent work of G. S. Klein and his associates on cognitive controls as structural variables: Gardner *et al.*, 1959). Drawing on this tradition and that of psychopathology generally, psychodiagnosis concerns itself with structural variables and their constellation into a limited number of ideal types (e.g., the obsessive-compulsive type of ego-structure) which, in the best practice, are used not as pigeonholes but as reference points in terms of which the clinician creates individualized analyses of personality structure.

6. *There can be no general laws of personality because of the role of chance and free will in human affairs.* There are hardly any contemporary personologists who openly espouse this argument. It played an important part in the development of the romantic point of view, as we have seen, and persists in Catholic psychology. It is generally admitted, however, that scientific work requires the basic assumption of strict determinism throughout. Closely examined, chance becomes ignorance; when we discover systematic effects where "error" existed before, the chance (at least in part) disappears. Theoretically, the exact path of a bolt of lightning and the exact events of a human life could be predicted rigorously, if we only had all of the necessary data at hand.

7. *General laws are not possible in personology because its subject matter is unique individuals, which have no place in natural science.* It is not difficult to dispose of this last, supposedly critical point of difference between *Naturwissenschaft* and *Geisteswissenschaft.*

The mechanistic, pre-field-theoretical science of Windelband's day contained a curious dictum that has been one of the principal sources of confusion on this whole issue: *Scientia non est individuorum*—science does not deal with individual cases. This hoary slogan dates back to the days when Aristotle was the last word on matters scientific, and the whole point of view it expresses is outdated in the physical sciences. According to this philosophy, the individual case was not lawful, since laws were conceived of as empirical regularities. This is the point of view (Plato's idealism or what Popper calls *essentialism*) that considers an average to be the only fact, and all deviation from it mere error.

Freud and Lewin have taught us that psychic determinism is thoroughgoing (see above), and the individual case is completely lawful. It is just difficult to know what the laws are from a study of one case, no matter how thorough. We can surmise (or, if you will, intuit) general laws from a single case in the hypothesis-forming phase of scientific endeavor, but we can verify them only by resorting to experimental or statistical inquiry or both.

There is truth in the old adage only in one sense, then: We cannot carry out the complete scientific process by the study of an individual. It is true that in certain of the disciplines concerned with man, from anatomy to sensory psychology, it has usually been assumed that the phenomena being studied are so universal that they can be located for study in any single person, and so autonomous from entanglement in idiosyncratically variable aspects of individuals that the findings of intensive investigation will have general applicability to people at large. Every so often, however, these assumptions turn out not to be tenable.

It is a mistake to focus personology on just those aspects of a person that are unique, as Weber (1949) saw clearly half a century ago. "The attempt to understand 'Bismarck,'" he said for example, "by leaving out of account everything which he has in common with other men and keeping what is 'particular' to him would be an instructive and amusing exercise for beginners. One would in that case . . . preserve, for example, as one of those 'finest flowers' [of such an analysis of uniqueness] his 'thumbprint,' that most specific indication of 'individuality.'" And some of the most critical points about him for predicting his behavior would have to be excluded because he shared them with other persons. Indeed, in contemporary psychodiagnosis, it is considered most useful to treat as a quantitative variable the degree to which a person's responses resemble those of the group as a whole.

The only kind of law that Allport could conceive for personology was one (like his principle of functional autonomy) that describes how uniqueness comes about. Personology has not been much restrained from seeking general relationships among its variables by this narrow view, however; the journals are full of investigations in which aspects of personality are studied genetically (that is, are related to the abstract variable of age) or are correlated, one with another. Once one treats uniqueness not with awe but with the casual familiarity due any other truistic fact of life, it ceases to pose any difficulty for personology.

Writing intensive case studies (on the genesis and structure of individual personalities) turns out not to be a particularly fruitful method, except for the generation of hypotheses. This is a very important exception, but the point is that personology does not proceed mainly by adding one exhaustive scientific biography to another, looking for generalizations afterwards. The Gestaltist taboo on studying any variable out of its context in the individual life is an overstatement. There is, of course, such a phenomenon as the interaction of variables, but it is not so far-reachingly prevalent as to make impossible any study of two variables at a time. As Falk (1956) has shown, the condition of interactive nonsummativeness is found in many other kinds of subject matter besides personality and creates no major difficulties of method or procedure.

In summary, in this section we have looked at the major propositions of the romantic point of view as applied to personology, and have found that the "basic differences" between this field and natural science are completely illusory. No basis for a separate methodology exists, and the objections to applying the general methodology of science to personalities turn out to be based on misunderstandings or on a narrow conception of natural science that is an anachronism today.

It by no means follows, as Eysenck (1954) puts it, that the science of personality should therefore be considered nomothetic. The nomothetic conception of science must be rejected as a caricature of what any contemporary scientist does. The only way to justify the application of the term nomothetic to the natural science of the present is to change the definition of the term so much that it no longer resembles its original meaning, and becomes an unnecessary redundancy. It can only lead to confusion to introduce such (unacknowledged) changes of definition; the nomothetic is as dead a duck today as the idiographic, and neither term adds anything to contemporary philosophy of science.

Many psychologists have followed Allport in taking the apparently sensible "middle position" of trying to deal with the objections that have been raised to his extreme idiographic pronouncements by saying, let's have a personology that is *both* nomothetic and idiographic (e.g., McClelland, 1951; MacKinnon, 1951). Thus, whenever he approaches the realization that the idiographic discipline of which he dreams is unworkable, Allport says, in effect, "I am not an extremist; common traits have their uses, even though they are only approximations, and personology can use both nomothetic and idiographic contributions." In practice, what this amounts to is that whenever attention is focused on individual cases, the inquiry is called idiographic, and otherwise it is considered nomothetic.

My objection to this "solution," this apparently reasonable compromise between antithetical positions, is that it is achieved only by a perversion of the original definitions, and that it accomplishes nothing except the preservation of a pair of pedantic words for our jargon. If one really accepts the arguments for an idiographic *Geisteswissenschaft* he can logically have no truck with nomothetic methods. They exist no longer, anyway, except in the history books; scientific method, as understood and practiced today in natural science and personology alike, is not a combination nor blend of nomothetic and idiographic approaches, but something bigger and better than both of them. The original dichotomies were badly formulated and based on misconceptions. The accompanying terminology might best be forgotten along with them.

Is There an Idiographic Method?

The last stand of the proponents of the romantic dichotomy is the contention that there are distinct generalizing (nomothetic) and individualizing (idiographic) *methods* in personology. This is the point of departure for Stephenson (1953), and some others who are enchanted by the mystique of *Q*. Inflating his ingenious rating technique into a whole so-called methodology, Stephenson has argued that his device of rating on an ipsative instead of a normative scale creates a specifically idiographic method for personology. When one *Q*-sorts a group of items for a subject, he makes a set of ratings which are forced into a normal distribution and scaled according to each item's applicability to this particular person (which is ipsative scaling, as opposed to the usual normative ratings where the standard is the distribution in a population of comparable persons). The device is clever and often useful; it enables a judge to give quantitative ratings to a great number of variables for one person without any reference to any sort of standard population; the population is intrapersonal (cf. Block, 1962).

Here is a technique suited to individual cases; is it therefore idiographic, something fundamentally different from conventional scientific methods of rating personality? Hardly. Actually, *Q*-sorts are typically used in large studies in which the individual case is an anonymous statistic. Moreover, it is a kind of Procrustean bed, imposing a standard pattern of ratings on every personality: all must have the same mean, standard deviation, and near-normal distribution. What is even further from the spirit of Allport's crusade for individual traits, the "items" are common traits, applied to everyone with no allowance for their failure to fit certain cases. In summary, then, the *Q*-sort is quite unacceptable in the traditional meaning of the term idiographic, and the use of that term to signify the fact that it is applied to individuals is simply a grandiloquent pose.

Following Allport (1942), others (e.g., Dymond, 1953; Hoffman, 1960) have revived the tired old terms either in an attempt to bolster, or in an attack on, the contention that clinical predictions must be superior to statistical predictions, because the clinician uses idiographic methods which alone are appropriate to predictions about individual cases. Here is another badly formulated pseudo-issue (Holt, 1958). Whether a clinician or a formula does better in making a particular kind of prediction is an empirical question, and one of little general interest. Clinicians and statisticians have their own proper spheres of activity, which overlap but little, and the difference between their activities has nothing to do with methodological issues. The method of clinical judgment has a great deal in common with the hypothesis-forming and theory-building phases of work in all the sciences (Holt, 1961).

In the end, we see that there is no need for a special type of science to be applied to individual personalities, and that the attempt to promulgate such a science fell into hopeless contradictions and absurdities. Today, Windelband's terms continue to appear in psychological writing but largely as pretentious jargon, mouth-filling polysyllables to awe the uninitiated, but never as essential concepts to make any scientifically vital point. Let us simply drop them from our vocabularies and let them die quietly.

Summary

The conception of two kinds of disciplines, a nomothetic science to study general principles and find abstract laws, and an idiographic science to study individuality, arose as a protest against a narrow conception of science in the nineteenth century. But the romantic movement of which it was a part started from fallacious premises, such as the conception that science is defined by its subject matter rather than its method, and its radical principles were never actually applied in pure form by any of its adherents. The idiographic point of view is an artistic one that strives for a nonscientific goal; the nomothetic, a caricature of science that bears little resemblance to anything that exists today. Since no useful purpose is served by retaining these mischievous and difficult terms, they had best disappear from our scientific vocabularies.

REFERENCES

Allport, G. W. *Personality, a psychological interpretation.* New York: Holt, 1937.

Allport, G. W. Motivation in personality: Reply to Mr. Bertocci. *Psychol. Rev.,* 1940, **47**, 533–554.

Allport, G. W. The use of personal documents in psychological science. *Soc. Sci. Res. Council Bull.,* 1942, **49**.

Allport, G. W. Personalistic psychology as science: A reply. *Psychol. Rev.,* 1946, **53**, 132–135.

Allport, G. W. *Becoming: Basic considerations for a psychology of personality.* New Haven: Yale Univ. Press, 1955.

Beck, S. J. The science of personality: Nomothetic or idiographic? *Psychol. Rev.,* 1953, **60**, 353–359.

Bellak, L. Freud and projective techniques. *J. proj. Tech.,* 1956, **20**, 5–13.

Bertalanffy, L. von. Theoretical models in biology and psychology. *J. Pers.,* 1951, **20**, 24–38.

Block, W. E. Psychometric aspects of the Rorschach technique. *J. proj. Tech.,* 1962, **26** (2), 162–172.

Colby, K. M. *A skeptical psychoanalyst.* New York: Wiley, 1958.

Dymond, Rosalind. Can clinicians predict individual behavior? *J. Pers.,* 1953, **22**, 151–161.

Eysenck, H. J. The science of personality: Nomothetic! *Psychol. Rev.,* 1954, **61**, 339–342.

Falk, J. L. Issues distinguishing nomothetic from idiographic approaches to personality theory. *Psychol. Rev.,* 1956, **63**, 53–62.

Freud, S. *The ego and the id.* London: Hogarth, 1947.

Gardner, R., Holzman, P. S., Klein, G. S., Linton, Harriet B., and Spence, D. P. Cognitive control: A study of individual consistencies in cognitive behavior. *Psychol. Issues,* 1959, **1**, No. 4.

Hoffman, P. J. The paramorphic representation of clinical judgment. *Psychol. Bull.,* 1960, **57**, 116–131.

Holt, R. R. Clinical and statistical prediction: A reformulation and some new data. *J. abnorm. soc. Psychol.,* 1958, **56**, 1–12.

Holt, R. R. Recent developments in psychoanalytic ego psychology and their implications for diagnostic testing. *J. proj. Tech.,* 1960, **24**, 254–266.

Holt, R. R. Clinical judgment as a disciplined inquiry. *J. nerv. ment. Dis.,* 1961, **133**, 369–382.

Klein, G. S., and Schlesinger, H. J. Where is the perceiver in perceptual theory? *J. Pers.,* 1949, **18**, 32–47.

McClelland, D. C. *Personality.* New York: Dryden Press, 1951.

MacKinnon, D. W. Personality. *Ann. Rev. Psychol.,* 1951, **2**, 113–136.

Murphy, G. *Personality: A biosocial approach to origins and structure.* New York: Harper, 1947.

Parsons, T. *The structure of social action.* Glencoe, Ill.: Free Press, 1957.

Rapaport, D., and Gill, M. M. The point of view and assumptions of metapsychology. *Int. J. Psychoanal.,* 1959, **40**, 153–162.

Sarbin, T. R. The logic of prediction in psychology. *Psychol. Rev.,* 1944, **51**, 210–228.

Stephenson, W. *The study of behavior: Q-technique and its methodology.* Chicago: Univ. of Chicago Press, 1953.

Weber, M. *The methodology of the social sciences.* (Trans. and ed. by E. A. Shils and H. A. Finch.) Glencoe, Ill.: Free Press, 1949. (The material collected here was originally published from 1904 to 1917.)

8

PSYCHOLOGY AS A PROFESSION

As a scientific discipline advances, its findings—whether or not the scientists intend it—are likely to become increasingly consequential in the world of practical affairs. Beginning with World War I, and especially since World War II, the development of applied psychology has been exceptionally rapid; and an increasing number of psychologists are becoming concerned primarily with professional (or applied) rather than purely scientific affairs.

When a science becomes recognized as useful and when individuals educated and trained in that science begin to render recompensable services to individuals, businesses, or to other nonacademic and nonresearch institutions, that science either spawns a separate profession (as physics spawned engineering) or it becomes a science-and-profession. Since about 1940, American psychology has existed as a science-and-profession, and as a social entity it is represented by the American Psychological Association. In this national organization, some individuals are concerned primarily with research, or the discovery of knowledge; others with teaching, or the dissemination of knowledge; and others are devoted primarily to the application of their knowledge in the solution of practical problems.

Whenever there is a move toward the application of knowledge, there must also be a concern for such matters as professional ethics, high standards for professional training, workable relationships with other professions, and a meaningful pattern of relationships with other institutions.

The following excerpts from an article by E. L. Hoch and John G. Darley deal—most often explicitly but sometimes only between the lines—with some facets of psychology as a profession. The article and the reality underlying it have implications for the future relation of psychology and psychologists to the courts. It bears on the relation between clinical psychology and psychiatry. It has a bearing also on whether all emotional disturbances are to be defined as illnesses and whether psychotherapy is to be established as a medical process.

Incidentally, but not inconsequentially, the article also describes the American Psychological Association, relates some of the history of American psychology, and mentions some of the training of clinical and other psychologists.

A CASE AT LAW*

E. L. Hoch and John G. Darley

On or about June 10, 1959, in the District of Columbia, Vincent E. Jenkins entered the home of Kenneth and Ann Joralemon. He was later arraigned in the United States District Court for the District of Columbia on charges of housebreaking with intent to commit an assault, assault with intent to steal, assault with intent to rape, and assault with a dangerous weapon.

As attorney for Mr. Jenkins, the court appointed Gerald Golin who, after the defendant had pleaded not guilty to the indictment, filed on July 7, 1959, a motion for mental examination of his client. July 9, 1959, found the latter committed to D.C. General Hospital for examination to determine his competence to stand trial. On motion of the Government, the trial court enlarged the commitment order on September 4, 1959, to have the examination include a determination of the defendant's mental condition on June 10, 1959, date of the alleged crime.

On November 27, 1959, a letter of November 25, 1959, from the Chief Psychiatrist of D.C. General Hospital was filed in the trial court stating that (a) defendant was incompetent to stand trial, and (b) he had been mentally incompetent on June 10, 1959. The Government entered no objections and, accordingly, on December 15, 1959, an order was filed committing Jenkins to St. Elizabeth's Hospital.

Some 10 months later, a letter of October 13, 1960, from the Superintendent of St. Elizabeth's Hospital was filed in the trial court to the effect that the defendant was now competent to stand trial.

* Abridged from *American Psychologist,* Vol. 17, 1962, pp. 623–654. By permission.

The attorney for the defense objected to the report, and a hearing was held at which only one witness (a psychiatrist) testified. In his opinion the defendant was competent to stand trial; he admitted, however, that the defendant had not recovered and was in essentially the same condition as on admission. Despite the objections entered by the attorney for the defense, the trial court ruled that his client was now competent to stand trial.

The trial of Mr. Jenkins began on January 23, 1961, and continued through January 30, 1961. The defense did not attempt to refute the fact that an attack had taken place. It based its case solely on grounds of insanity and placed in evidence the testimony of four lay witnesses, two psychiatrists, and three psychologists.

The lay witnesses all cited instances of unusual behavior on his part over the years. The Chief Psychiatrist of D.C. General Hospital testified that she had originally diagnosed the defendant as suffering from a mental defect (on the basis of psychological test results and her personal examinations); she now felt, on the basis of further evidence, that he was suffering from a mental disease and that the crime had been a product of mental disease. On its own initiative, the trial court ordered stricken from the record any testimony by the psychiatrist to the effect that the defendant was schizophrenic on June 10, 1959.

The Assistant Chief Psychiatrist of D.C. General Hospital, a second witness for the defense, testified on the basis of his four examinations between September and December, 1959, that the defendant was suffering from both mental retardation and a chronic undifferentiated psychosis. Again on its own initiative, the trial court later excluded any testimony that the defendant was suffering from an undifferentiated psychosis as not based upon proper evidence.

The court accepted as qualified the three psychologists whose testimony was entered in evidence by the attorney for the defense. In the opinion of the Chief Psychologist of D.C. General Hospital and the Chief Psychologist and a staff psychologist of St. Elizabeth's Hospital, the defendant was schizophrenic and had been so at the time of the alleged crime.

In rebuttal, the prosecution (Government) presented two psychiatrists from the staff of St. Elizabeth's Hospital. Neither found the defendant to have been suffering from mental disease or defect on June 10, 1959.

In instructing the jury, the trial court added:

The Court also holds that a psychologist is not competent to give a medical opinion as to a mental disease or a mental defect. Therefore, you will not consider any evidence to the effect that the defendant was suffering from a mental disease or a mental defect on June 10, 1959, according to the testimony given by the psychologists.

The jury found Mr. Jenkins guilty on all counts except that of intent to steal, and on March 10, 1961, the Court sentenced him to imprisonment for 5 to 15 years.

On May 29, 1961, the attorney for the defense filed in the United States Court of Appeals for the District of Columbia Circuit the brief of an appeal from the decision of the trial court. The argument was based on four grounds:

1. The trial court, having originally found appellant incompetent to stand trial, erred in later finding him competent in the absence of satisfactory evidence of restoration to mental competency.
2. The trial court erred in having ordered stricken from the record, or excluded, the testimony of the two psychiatrists for the defense to the effect that appellant was suffering from an undifferentiated psychosis or mental disease.
3. The manner in which the trial court had examined the expert witnesses for the defense had been severely prejudicial to appellant and deprived him of his right to a fair and impartial trial by jury.
4. The trial court erred in instructing the jury to disregard the testimony of the psychologists concerning appellant's mental condition.

Consequently, the attorney for the appellant concluded, the case should be reversed and remanded with instructions to place Mr. Jenkins in St. Elizabeth's Hospital until such time as it might be certified that the latter had been restored to mental competency; or the case should be reversed and remanded and a new trial awarded the defendant.

At this time, through the liaison efforts of one of the psychologists who had been involved in the trial, counsel for the appellant was invited to the APA [American Psychological Association] Central Office. Of mutual concern was the question of whether the Association should consider the possibility of filing a brief as *amicus curiae*. In his letter of May 31, 1961, to the Association's general counsel enclosing relevant background materials, the Executive Officer requested advice with respect to: (a) the estimated probability of the case's turning on the issue of psychologists' qualifications as expert witnesses; (b) the possible precedent-setting significance of the outcome of such a case in this particular jurisdiction; (c) the projected cost to the Association of preparing a brief and possible oral argument.

APA's counsel pointed out the following in his reply of June 20, 1961, to the Executive Officer:

1. The matter in which APA was specifically interested (qualification of psychologists as expert witnesses) was not the only issue in the case. Therefore, the case could conceivably be decided without ever reaching the particular issue with which APA was primarily concerned.

2. At the time the trial judge gave the allegedly prejudicial instruction to the jury (to disregard the testimony of the psychologists), counsel for the appellant did not object to the instruction about which complaint was now being made. Under Rule 30 of the *Federal Rules of Criminal Procedure,* such objection and the grounds therefor must be distinctly stated before the jury retires to consider its verdict. There have been many decisions by federal courts refusing to consider an alleged error in an instruction when an objection had not been made in the trial court. The Court of Appeals might consider the issue nevertheless in the present instance; whether it would decide to do so was, however, conjectural.

3. If, mindful of the possibilities noted under 1 and 2 above, APA wished still to file an *amicus curiae* brief, the cost to the Association of the necessary legal preparation would run to several thousand dollars.

Under the circumstances, the calculated risk of not filing a brief as *amicus curiae* was taken. At the same time, the attorney for the appellant was assured that he could count on the APA Central Office for whatever assistance might appropriately be furnished.

On October 26, 1961, the United States Court of Appeals for the District of Columbia Circuit handed down a 2-to-1 decision (by Judges Bazelon and Fahy, Judge Bastian dissenting) which reversed the decision of the lower court and remanded the case for a new trial. The opinion spoke also to the issue of concern to APA and ruled in favor of psychologists as expert witnesses. (A full account of the decision has been reported earlier (*Amer. Psychologist,* 1961, **16**, 718–719).)

On December 12, 1961, the Government filed a Petition for Rehearing *En Banc* (before the full nine-man Court of Appeals). This time it was clear that the Government would not challenge the result insofar as the defendant was concerned but that the point of law in question was the one in which psychology had a compelling stake, namely, the validity of the testimony of psychologists.

The *Washington Post* of January 16, 1962, carried the news that the United States Court of Appeals had on the preceding day decided to hear the appeal by the Government. In a letter of the same date, the Executive Officer requested the APA general counsel to undertake preparation of an *amicus curiae* brief for presentation to the full nine-man Court of Appeals. The central and only issue this time, the one to which the Court ordered the rehearing *en banc* limited, was the correctness of

> . . . the ruling of the District Court which excluded from consideration by the jury the testimony of the psychologist concerning the existence and effects of the "mental disease or defect."

With the APA Central Office staff serving as "co-authors" with its legal counsel, the legal machinery was set in motion. A letter of January 18, 1962, from the attorney for the appellant granted APA counsel the necessary consent to file a brief as *amicus curiae* and further agreed that, should the Court allow oral argument, the attorneys for APA could present oral argument. On January 19, 1962, APA legal counsel filed with the United States Court of Appeals a Motion for Leave to File Brief as *Amicus Curiae,* indicating that the necessary consent of the attorney for the appellant had been obtained and that the United States Attorney's Office had interposed no objection.

> Comes now the American Psychological Association, by and through its attorneys, Arthur B. Hanson and Samuel J. L'Hommedieu, Jr., and moves to file a brief as *amicus curiae* on or before February 19, 1962, for the reasons hereinafter set forth.
>
> The reasons:
>
> The American Psychological Association has a vital interest in this issue. This Association is the only national association representing the discipline of Psychology. It was founded in 1892 and incorporated in the District of Columbia in 1925 as a nonprofit organization and presently has approximately 20,000 members. It publishes 12 psychological journals and is composed of 20 divisions. . . .

The motion was granted. A further Motion for Leave to Argue, which requested ". . . that the American Psychological Association be permitted thirty (30) minutes' time in which to argue the case as *amicus curiae*" was denied.

The first draft of the prospective brief reached APA on the evening of January 30, 1962, was reviewed by the Executive Officer that night, and became the day's only order of business on January 31. Responsibility for reviewing and editing various sections of the draft was assigned to senior staff members.

The authors met the evening of January 31 with APA's legal counsel and two members of his staff, and three psychologists who had testified in the case, and a fourth psychologist of considerable experience in legal settings, to revise the draft of the brief. The same group held a second late-night meeting on February 7, 1962, the day on which the revised draft appeared in print and was filed, this time joined by the court-appointed defense attorney. Here the focus was on briefing the latter on psychological rather than legal aspects, the motion for oral argument having been denied the APA legal staff.

On February 8, 1962, the eve of the rehearing *en banc,* material detailing specifically the functions, qualifications, and program of training of clinical psychologists was prepared for and delivered to counsel for the appellant.

Thirty minutes before the opening "Oyez!" on the morning of February 9, 1962, several members of the APA staff, other interested psychologists, and a number of additional spectators filled the available seats in the dignified chamber of the United States Court of Appeals. Seated on the working side of the rail were the opposing attorneys and their supporting legal talent, among them the general counsel for APA and his staff.

Another event had taken place shortly before the rehearing *en banc*. On February 7, 1962, the American Psychiatric Association submitted a Motion for Leave to file a brief as *amicus curiae* and to participate in the oral argument. Chief Judge Miller, on February 8, 1962, entered an order allowing until February 23, 1962, for the filing of the brief but denying permission for oral argument. On February 23, 1962, the American Psychiatric Association filed its brief, after hearing the oral arguments presented to the court and studying the brief prepared by the APA.

The final written opinion in the case was handed down June 7, 1962. It sustains, by a 7–2 vote, the acceptability of testimony by properly qualified psychologists in cases involving the determination and meaning of mental disease or defect as productive of criminal acts.

Following this condensed narrative of events, we present now, in their entirety,* the *amicus curiae* briefs of the American Psychological Association and the American Psychiatric Association, together with the opinion of the full court, rendered June 7, 1962.

Readers who are familiar with our long history of relationships with psychiatry and our policy positions on interprofessional relations and ethics may find these documents of considerable interest. Whether our labyrinthine involvement with the legal process in this case will be a true historic landmark, or, in the words of Robert Southey, merely "a famous victory,"[1] remains to be seen.

Statement of the Case

In the Court below, defendant was convicted of the crimes of housebreaking with intent to commit an assault, assault with intent to rape, and assault with a dangerous weapon. At the trial, defendant relied solely upon the defense of insanity. In support of this defense, defendant presented the testimony, *inter alia,* of three clinical psychologists with from three to twenty-five years' clinical experience, who had received Ph.D. degrees in institutions approved for clinical training by the American Psychological Association.

One of these three was the Chief Psychologist of St. Elizabeth's Hospital; one was the Chief Psychologist of the District of Columbia General Hospital; and the third was a psychologist on the Staff of St. Elizabeth's Hospital at the time he examined the defendant.

Upon the basis of personal contact with the defendant, review of his case history, and upon the basis of the results of standard psychological tests administered by these psychologists or under their direction, they all testified that on the date the alleged crimes were committed, defendant had been suffering from schizophrenia. One of the three testified that he could give no opinion concerning the relationship between the illness and the crimes but the other two gave it as their opinions, respectively, that the disease and the crimes were "related," and that the crimes were the product of the illness.

* Only excerpts from the original briefs are presented here.—Ed.

[1] Robert Southey's "Battle of Blenheim":

> "But what good came of it at last?"
> Quoth little Peterkin.
> "Why, that I cannot tell," said he;
> "But 'twas a famous victory."

At the conclusion of the trial, the judge instructed the jury to disregard the opinions of the psychologists.

On appeal to this Court from the conviction, the panel of the Court which heard the case held, *inter alia,* one judge dissenting, that the Trial Court had committed reversible error in excluding the expert opinions of the psychologists.

Upon motion of the Government, the Court ordered a rehearing *en banc* limited to the issue of the correctness of

> . . . the ruling of the District Court which excluded from consideration by the jury the testimony of the psychologist concerning the existence and effects of the "mental disease or defect."

By motion filed January 15, 1962, the American Psychological Association sought leave to file this brief *amicus curiae* with respect to the issue stated above. Neither appellant nor appellee opposed the motion and the Court granted it by order dated January 29, 1962.

Statement of Interest of Amicus Curiae

The American Psychological Association, hereinafter sometimes referred to as "the Association," is the only national membership organization of the profession and science of psychology. As such it has a vital interest in endeavoring to aid the Court in reaching a correct understanding of and decision upon the issue presented in this rehearing.

The Association has been in continuous existence since its foundation in 1892. At present the Association has in excess of 20,000 members, which number includes a majority of the qualified psychologists in this country.

There are three classes of membership in the Association, namely, Fellows, Members, and Associates.

The minimum standards for Fellow status are (a) a doctoral degree based in part upon a psychological dissertation conferred by a graduate school of recognized standing, (b) prior status as a Member for at least one year, (c) active engagement at the time of nomination in the advancement of psychology in any of its aspects, (d) five years of acceptable professional experience subsequent to the granting of the doctoral degree, and (e) evidence of unusual and outstanding contribution or performance in the field of psychology.

The minimum standard for election to Member status is the receipt of the doctoral degree based in part upon a psychological dissertation and conferred by a graduate school of recognized standing. In addition, candidates for Member status must be engaged in study or professional work that is primarily psychological in nature.

The minimum standard for election to Associate status is: (a) completion of at least two years of graduate work in psychology in a recognized graduate school, or (b) the Master's degree in psychology from a recognized graduate school plus a year of acceptable experience in professional work that is psychological in nature. In addition, candidates for Associate status must be devoting full time to professional or graduate work that is primarily psychological in nature.

Only those having the status of Fellows or Members are eligible to vote or hold office in the Association.

The purposes of the Association, as stated in Article I of its Bylaws, are as follows:

1. The objects of the American Psychological Association shall be to advance psychology as a science and as a means of promoting human welfare by the encouragement of psychology in all its branches in the broadest and most liberal manner; by the promotion of research in psychology and the improvement of research methods and conditions; by the improvement of the qualifications and usefulness of psychologists through high standards of professional ethics, conduct, education, and achievement; by the increase and diffusion of psychological knowledge through meetings, professional contacts, reports, papers, discussions, and publications; thereby to advance scientific interests and inquiry, and the application of research findings to the promotion of public welfare.

Article V of the Association's Bylaws provides for the creation of Divisions within the Association to represent major scientific and professional interests in the general field of psychology. At present there are twenty such Divisions within the Association. They are:

Division of General Psychology
Division on the Teaching of Psychology
Division of Experimental Psychology
Division on Evaluation and Measurement
Division on Developmental Psychology
Division of Personality and Social Psychology
The Society for the Psychological Study of Social Issues—A Division of the APA

Division of Industrial and Business Psychology
Division of Educational Psychology
Division of School Psychologists
Division of Counseling Psychology
Division of Psychologists in Public Service
Division on Esthetics
Division of Clinical Psychology
Division of Consulting Psychology
Division on Military Psychology
Division on Maturity and Old Age
The Society of Engineering Psychologists—A Division of the APA
National Council on Psychological Aspects of Disability—A Division of the APA
Division of Consumer Psychology

The psychologists whose testimony is the subject of this rehearing are members of the Association. In addition, one is a Member of the Division of Clinical Psychology; another a Fellow of that Division, as well as a Fellow of the Association. The latter (the Chief Psychologist of St. Elizabeth's Hospital) is also a Diplomate of the American Board of Examiners in Professional Psychology—a mark of professional standing of which more will be said in Part IV, B, of this brief.

Summary of Argument

1. A qualified psychologist is competent to state, as an expert witness, his professional opinion upon matters within the scope of his qualifications.

2. A clinical psychologist is competent in a criminal proceeding to give an expert professional opinion as to the nature of and the existence or non-existence of mental disease or defect in the accused and as to the causal relationship or lack thereof, between such mental disease or defect and the crime or crimes for which the accused is on trial.

3. In the case at bar, the panel which first heard this appeal properly held that the Trial Judge committed error when he excluded from the Jury's consideration the testimony of the psychologists as to the mental condition of the defendant on the day of the crimes, and the causal relationship between his mental condition and the crimes of which he was on trial.

Argument A:
Psychology Is an Established Science

In any inquiry as to the testimonial competence of a psychologist to express an expert professional opinion, it is important to understand that psychology is an established science which makes use of the same fundamental methods of investigation and inquiry and the same criteria of objectivity and thoroughness as are used in all recognized scientific disciplines.

Psychology, the science of human behavior, has its origins in many areas of inquiry. It grew in part from the great philosophical concerns with human behavior and conduct. Its immediate origins as a science, however, can be placed in the period of scientific development in the mid-nineteenth century. It was at the University of Leipzig in 1879 that Professor Wilhelm Wundt established the first laboratory in scientific psychology. Since that time the major emphasis in the development of psychology has been along scientific lines, with increased application of the results of research to a wide variety of problems of human behavior.

It is interesting to note that the first intelligence test, the derivatives of which are so widely used today in education, industry, government, and institutions, was developed in 1905 by Alfred Binet, a French psychologist who was Director of the Psychological Laboratory at the Sorbonne. The first American adaptation of this test was published the same year, but the 1916 Stanford Revision set the pattern for the measurement of mental ability throughout the United States. Further modified in 1937 as the Revised Stanford-Binet Scale, and again modified in 1960, this test continues to be extensively used today.

From a scholarly discipline and science developed mainly in university centers, the result of psychological effort has become recognized as capable of application in many fields of human activity. In the interval between the two World Wars, applications were taking place in business and industry and in education. During World War II, the methods and techniques developed by psychologists found extensive application in the wide range of events covered by the war years, and played a vital role in the recruitment, selection, classification, assignment, and training of individuals accepted for military service. Newer applications of psychology were possible in such areas as psychological warfare, aviation and submarine operations, treatment of casualties and offenders, design of equipment, such as radar, with a view towards the best utilization of the skills of the human operator, food and nutrition research, the effect of drugs on behavior, morale and productivity of groups, and a host of other problems. Since World War II, new and vitally important practical uses of the skills of psychologists have taken place at a remarkable rate.

The foundation stone, however, of all developments of the field continues to be a rigid adherence to the principles of science, to a belief in the value of empirical evidence and verification, and to the development of appropriate theory. These are some of the processes which differentiate the sciences from other approaches to the understanding of human behavior.

Conclusion

In light of the foregoing it is clear that psychology is an established science and profession. It is also clear that psychologists are highly trained experts in their profession. As an adjunct to these conclusions it is also clear that the clinical psychologist, through systematic professional training and through professional experience, is qualified to formulate and express expert professional opinions in the field of mental disease and mental defect.

By reason of this professional competence, it is submitted that the clinical psychologist is fully qualified under the established legal principles governing competence of expert witnesses, to express a professional expert opinion in criminal cases upon the issues governing criminal responsibility under the *Durham* rule.

For these reasons it is respectfully urged that the issue presented upon this rehearing was correctly decided by the panel of this Court that first heard this appeal. . . .

Statement of Interest and Position of the American Psychiatric Association

The American Psychiatric Association, founded in 1844, is the national membership organization of Doctors of Medicine who specialize in the diagnosis, treatment and care of mental illnesses. Doctors of Medicine who qualify and specialize in the field of mental illness are psychiatrists and alienists. The Association is comprised of those twelve thousand qualified Doctors of Medicine who specialize and practice as psychiatrists.

Psychiatrists traditionally have been called upon by our Courts to give expert medical testimony concerning mental illnesses, the productivity thereof and their effects.

The question of whether a person *not* trained in medicine, *not* a Doctor of Medicine and *not* a doctor trained as a specialist in the diagnosis, treatment and care of the mentally ill, can qualify as a *medical* expert and give expert *medical* opinions concerning the diagnosis of specific mental diseases and the *medical* effects thereof is of grave concern to psychiatrists and their Association.

Psychiatrists, or alienists as they have also been termed in times past, are qualified Doctors of Medicine who specialize in the diagnosis, care and treatment of mental illnesses (Webster's International and Concise Dictionaries). Briefly, the psychiatrist now receives a minimum of thirteen years of medical training and special experience, needed to qualify a Doctor of Medicine as a Psychiatrist. This special training in medicine is discussed later in the brief.

A psychologist is not so trained. The psychologists, testifying below —as found by the Trial Judge and by the majority of the panel in its decision (S.O. p. 10)—"lack medical training." A reading of the brief of the American Psychological Association (pp. 3–18) will show that psychologists are trained in the "science of psychology." Psychology basically deals with philosophy. Psychologists study philosophy, not medicine, and their objectives as stated in the "purposes" of their Association, "shall be to advance psychology (not medicine) . . . . as a means of promoting human welfare . . . " (Brief, p. 4).

In the Divisions created by the American Psychological Association, some twenty in number, none deal with medical diagnosis, treatment and care of mental illnesses (Brief, p. 5). The nearest approach to mental illness and its effects is a category called "Division of Clinical Psychology." As the psychologists who testified at the trial had some experience as clinical psychologists, let us comment on the part the clinical psychologist plays in the diagnosis and treatment of the mentally ill. These psychologists studied philosophy, not medicine, and have Ph.D. degrees, i.e., Doctors of Philosophy. The clinical psychologist, like "teachers, ministers, lawyers, social workers and vocational counselors," all utilize their skills as aids only to the psychiatrist in his medical diagnosis, care and treatment of the mentally ill. That the clinical psychologist only passes on his contribution as a part of the medical picture to be evaluated only by a qualified psychiatrist, was resolved by a Resolution on the Relationship of Psychotherapy to Medicine, approved by the Board of Trustees of the American Medical Association, the Council of the American Psychiatric Association, and the Executive Council of the American Psychoanalytical Association in 1954. This joint Resolution reads as follows:

For centuries the Western world has placed on the medical profession responsibility for the diagnosis and treatment of illness. Medical practice acts have been designed to protect the public from unqualified practitioners and to define the special responsibilities assumed by those who practice the healing art, for much harm may be done by unqualified persons, however good their intentions may be. To do justice to the patient requires the capacity to make a diagnosis and to prescribe appropriate treatment. Diagnosis often requires the ability to compare and contrast various diseases and disorders that have similar symptoms but different causes. Diagnosis is a continuing process, for the character of the illness changes with its treatment or with the passage of time, and that treatment which is appropriate may change accordingly.

Recognized medical training today involves, as a minimum, graduation from an approved medical school and internship in a hospital. Most physicians today receive additional medical training, and specialization requires still further training.

Psychiatry is the medical specialty concerned with illness that has chiefly mental symptoms. The psychiatrist is also concerned with mental causes of physical illness, for we have come to recognize that physical symptoms may have mental causes just as mental symptoms may have physical causes. The psychiatrist, with or without consultation with other physicians, must select from the many different methods of treatment at his disposal those methods that he considers appropriate to the particular patient. His treatment may be medicinal or surgical, physical (as electroshock) or psychological. The systematic application of the methods of psychological medicine to the treatment of illness, particularly as these methods involve gaining an understanding of the emotional state of the patient and aiding him to understand himself, is called psychotherapy. This special form of medical treatment may be highly developed, but it remains simply one of the possible methods of treatment to be selected for use according to medical criteria for use when it is indicated. Psychotherapy is a form of medical treatment and does not form the basis for a separate profession.

Other professional groups such as psychologists, teachers, ministers, lawyers, social workers, and vocational counselors, of course, use psychological understanding in carrying out their professional functions. Members of these professional groups are not thereby practicing medicine. The application of psychological methods to the treatment of illness is a medical function. Any physician may utilize the skills of others in his professional work, but he remains responsible, legally and morally, for the diagnosis and for the treatment of his patient.

The medical profession fully endorses the appropriate utilization of the skills of psychologists, social workers, and other professional personnel in contributing roles in settings directly supervised by physicians. It further recognizes that these professions are entirely independent and autonomous when medical questions are not involved; but when members of these professions contribute to the diagnosis and treatment of illness, their professional contributions must be coordinated under medical responsibility.

Reduced to simple terms, clinical psychology "remains simply one of the possible methods" to be selected by the psychiatrist in evaluating and treating a specific mental illness. Its use in any specific case is for the psychiatrist to determine, because this is a medical function reserved by joint agreement of the American Medical Association, the American Psychiatric Association and the American Psychoanalytical Association to the qualified psychiatrist. As their joint Resolution expresses this principle, "For centuries the Western world has placed on the *medical* profession responsibility for the diagnosis and treatment of illness" and "Psychiatry is the *medical* specialty concerned with illness that has chiefly mental symptoms" (italics supplied).

Summary of Argument

I. Psychiatrists undergo a minimum of thirteen years of special training and experience to qualify as a medical expert in the mental health field. The psychologists who testified below lack such medical training and experience, hence they are not medical experts in the mental health field. While they are skilled in psychology, this does not qualify them to diagnose or to prescribe treatment and care for a specific mental illness. Traditionally, ultimate medical diagnosis, care and treatment for the mentally ill is reserved to the psychiatrist.

The diagnosis of mental illness should be based on the *synthesis* of data from several sources. One source could be observations of and tests given by a clinical psychologist under direct medical supervision, but this is but a part of the history. Diagnosis to be ultimate must be made by a medical specialist, the psychiatrist, and psychological data plays only a part in this diagnosis. A clinical psychologist lacking medical training and experience is not qualified as a medical expert in this field and cannot diagnose, prescribe care and treatment of a specific case of mental illness, or give expert medical opinions on these end results. Traditionally, medical men have been relied upon by our Courts for expert testimony in medical fields.

II. The clinical psychologists who testified below admittedly are not educated, trained and experienced in medicine. They are not graduates of medical schools. They are not Doctors of Medicine. They are not psychiatrists or alienists. Traditionally, it is the primary function of the trial judge to pass upon the qualifications of any purported expert witness and to decide if expert testimony can be given in a particular instance. Here the instance was the giving of expert testimony concerning the existence of a specific mental illness in Appellant, its diagnosis, its productivity and the relationship of the particular mental illness to the criminal acts of Appellant. While the Trial Judge permitted the psychologists to testify to their observations and the various tests given to the Appellant, in exercising his sound discretion, he excluded expert medical opinions of these psychologists "as to a mental disease or defect," obviously, as the majority pointed out in the decision of October 26, 1961, "because psychologists lack medical training" (S.O. p. 10). The Trial Judge's decision was correct and certainly was not an abuse of his discretion.

III. The positions urged by the American Psychological Association's brief *amicus curiae* that (Brief, p. 8) "psychology is a learned profession," hence (Brief, p. 13) a "clinical psychologist is competent to express professional opinions upon the existence or non-existence of mental disease or defect and upon their causal relationships to overt behavior" are unsound.

Conclusion

The question of medical competence was for the Trial Judge. His decision on the competence of the psychologists or lack of it, was traditionally in his sound discretion, and that decision is conclusive, unless clearly erroneous as a matter of law (*Inland & Seaboard Coasting Co.* v. *Tolson,* 139 U.S. 55, *Hamilton* v. *United States,* 26 App. D.C. 391, 392). The learned Trial Judge's ruling that the psychologists who testified at the trial were not competent to give medical opinions as to a mental disease or a mental defect, because they lacked medical training and were neither doctors of medicine nor psychiatrists was correct, was not error nor an abuse of discretion. It is submitted that Judge Curran's ruling on this aspect of this appeal should be affirmed. . . .

Admissibility of the Psychologists' Opinions*

The next assignment of error we discuss concerns the court's instruction to the jury to disregard testimony of three defense psycholo-

* Excerpted from the majority opinion of the court.—Ed.

gists that appellant had a mental disease when he committed the crimes charged. Although appellant failed to object to this instruction, we consider it because it presents a question which is likely to arise upon a new trial.

The first psychologist, Dr. Tirnauer, administered a battery of tests to appellant, studied his case history, and concluded he had been suffering from schizophrenia when he committed the crimes. In his opinion, the disease and the crimes were "related." The second psychologist, Dr. Margaret Ives, had reviewed Dr. Tirnauer's test results, had seen appellant at a staff conference, and had administered part of a Szondi profile test. She stated that appellant was suffering from schizophrenia and that his crimes were the product of the disease. The third psychologist, Dr. Levy, interpreted test results obtained by members of the District General staff in October 1959, and administered two additional tests shortly before trial. He testified that defendant had been suffering from schizophrenia on June 10, 1959, but could give no opinion concerning the relationship between the illness and the crimes. At the conclusion of the trial the court instructed the jury:

> A psychologist is not competent to give a medical opinion as to a mental disease or defect. Therefore, you will not consider any evidence to the effect that the defendant was suffering from a mental disease or a mental defect on June 10, 1959, according to the testimony given by the psychologists.

The trial court apparently excluded these opinions because psychologists lack medical training. We agree with the weight of authority, however, that some psychologists are qualified to render expert testimony in the field of mental disorder.

We begin by placing this problem in the context of the considerations governing the reception of expert testimony.

> An observer is qualified to testify because he has first-hand knowledge which the jury does not have of the situation or transaction at issue. The expert has something different to contribute. This is a power to draw inferences from the facts which a jury would not be competent to draw. To warrant the use of expert testimony, then, two elements are required. First, the subject of the inference must be so distinctively related to some

science, profession, business or occupation as to be beyond the ken of the average layman, and second, the witness must have such skill, knowledge or experience in that field or calling as to make it appear that his opinion or inference will probably aid the trier in his search for truth. The knowledge may in some fields be derived from reading alone, in some from practice alone, or as is more commonly the case, from both. [McCormick, *Evidence* §13 (1954), citing authorities.]

The test, then, is whether the opinion offered will be likely to aid the trier in the search for truth. In light of that purpose, it is hardly surprising that courts do not exclude all but the very best kind of witness. See 2 Wigmore, *Evidence* § 569 (3d ed. 1940). Accord: *Fightmaster* v. *Mode,* 31 Ohio App. 273, 167 N.E. 407 (1928). Thus a general practitioner may testify concerning matters within a medical specialty if his education or experience, or both, involves demonstrable knowledge of the subject. *Sher* v. *DeHaven,* 91 U.S. App. D.C. 257, 199 F.2d 777 (1952), *cert. denied,* 345 U.S. 936 (1953); 2 Wigmore, *op. cit. supra.* Nor need a skilled witness on a medical subject be duly licensed to practice medicine. *Ibid.* The general rule is that "anyone who is shown to have special knowledge and skill in diagnosing and treating human ailments is qualified to testify as an expert, if his learning and training show that he is qualified to give an opinion on the particular question at issue." "It is not essential that the witness be a medical practitioner." 32 C.J.S. *Evidence* § 537 (1942). Thus, non-medical witnesses who have had experience in electrical work may testify to the effects of electrical shock upon the human body. *Vessels* v. *Kansas City Light & Power Co.,* 219 S.W. 80 (Mo. Sup. Ct. 1920); *Blakeney* v. *Alabama Power Co.,* 222 Ala. 394, 133 So. 16 (1931). Optometrists, whose training includes instruction in the symptoms of certain eye diseases, may testify to the presence of cataract discovered in the course of fitting glasses, *Jackson* v. *Waller,* 126 Comm. 295, 10 A.2d 763 (1940), and to the effect of a scar upon vision. *Black Starr Coal Corp.* v. *Reeder,* 278 Ky. 532, 128 S.W. 2d 905 (1939). A toxicologist has been permitted to testify to the effect of oxalic acid, a poison, upon the human eye. *Reynolds* v. *Davis,* 55 R.I. 206, 179 A. 613 (1935). The kinds of witnesses whose opinions courts have received, *even though they lacked medical training and would not be permitted by law to treat the conditions they described, are legion.* The principle to be distilled from the cases is plain: if experience or training enables a proffered expert witness to form an opinion which would aid the jury, in the absence of some countervailing consideration, his testimony will be received.

Suggesting the diagnostic category into which an accused's condition fits and relating it to his past behavior require skill far in excess of that possessed by laymen. Lest the jury be misled into relying on opinions which are not based upon relevant learning and experience, we must examine the reality behind the title "psychologist." Many psychologists may not qualify to testify concerning mental disease or defect. Their training and experience may not provide an adequate basis for their testimony. Some psychologists, for example, teach and engage in theoretical research in fields unrelated to the diagnosis and treatment of mental disease. Others are employed in personnel administration, still others advise industry on problems of employee morale. See Western Personnel Institute, *Opportunities for Psychologists, Psychiatrists, Psychiatric Social Workers,* 8–10 (1958); Daniel and Louttit, *Professional Problems in Psychology,* 250–52, 297 (1953). Such experience does not ordinarily provide the skill essential to offer expert testimony concerning mental disorders. *Cf.* Albee, *Mental Health Manpower Trends,* 116 (1959). Some psychologists, moreover, have had no post-graduate instruction. *Id.* at 121–22.

On the other hand, the Ph.D. in Clinical Psychology involves some —and often much—training and experience in the diagnosis and treatment of mental disorders. Typically, candidates are trained, *inter alia,* in general psychology, theory of personality and psychodynamics, psychopathology, diagnostic methods, therapeutic techniques, selected aspects of physiology and anatomy, and clinical methods. A one-year internship in a mental hospital is required for this degree. After graduation, many clinical psychologists administer and interpret diagnostic tests which elicit the patient's intellectual level, defenses, personality structure, attitudes, feelings, thought and perceptual processes. See 1 Rapaport, *Diagnostic Testing* 7–9 (1945). In many institutions and clinics their reports, which regularly include opinions concerning the presence or absence of mental disease or defect, are important aids to psychiatrists who customarily have the final responsibility for diagnosis. Some psychologists, moreover, regularly administer psychotherapy and related non-organic therapies in the treatment of certain types of mental disorders.

The determination of a psychologist's competence to render an expert opinion based on his findings as to the presence or absence of mental disease or defect must depend upon the nature and extent of his knowledge. It does not depend upon his claim to the title "psychologist." And that determination, after hearing, must be left in each case to the traditional discretion of the trial court subject to appellate review. Although there are no statutory criteria for licensing psychologists in the District of Columbia to assist trial courts, the American Psychological Association's list of approved graduate training programs provides some guidance. When completion of such training is followed by actual experience in the treatment and diagnosis of disease in association with psychiatrists or neurologists, the opinion of the psychologist may properly be received in evidence.

Some graduate clinical psychologists, moreover, are certified by the American Board of Examiners in Professional Psychology. Certification, which indicates exceptional professional competence, is awarded upon completion of written and oral examination in *inter alia,* diagnosis and treatment. Applicants must have four years, acceptable professional experience and must present credentials, including a sample of their work and letters of recommendation, showing sufficient professional achievement to warrant further examination. The purpose of Board certification is to identify and evaluate psychologists at an advanced professional level. If the post-doctoral experience required for certification has included substantial experience in a hospital or clinical setting in association with psychiatrists or neurologists, clinical psychologists who are diplomates of the American Board of Examiners in Professional Psychology should ordinarily qualify as expert witnesses.

We need not decide whether the three psychologists who testified for the defense at the trial under review were qualified to offer expert opinions since they may not be called to testify at the retrial. We hold only that the lack of a medical degree, and the lesser degree of responsibility for patient care which mental hospitals usually assign to psychologists, are not automatic disqualifications. Where relevant, these matters may be shown to affect the weight of their testimony, even though it be admitted in evidence. The critical factor in respect to admissibility is the actual experience of the witness and the probable probative value of his opinion. The trial judge should make a finding in respect to the individual qualifications of each challenged expert. Qualifications to express an opinion on a given topic are to be decided by the judge alone. The weight to be given any expert opinion admitted in evidence by the judge is exclusively for the jury.

GLOSSARY*

Anxiety. An unpleasant emotional state, subjectively experienced as a fusion of fear with the anticipation of future evil, in which a present and continuing strong desire or drive seems likely to miss its goal.

Associationism. A theory that starts with supposedly irreducible mental elements and asserts that learning and the development of higher processes consist mainly in the combination of these elements.

Asymptote. A straight line which a regular curve constantly approaches but never reaches, or reaches only at infinity.

Behaviorism. The view that psychology as a science studies only behavior. The basic contention of behaviorists has been that only the objectively observable can be the data of science. For this reason, consciousness was excluded (since it is usually defined as subjective), or it was held to be only a sort of covert language response.

Cognition. A generic term for any process whereby an organism becomes aware or obtains knowledge of an object. It includes perceiving, recognizing, conceiving, judging, reasoning.

Consensus. 1. A working together of more than one sense; the information gained by such a combination; e.g., that of taste and smell to yield flavor. 2. A decision participated in by all the members of a group and representing the maximum area of common acceptance.

Cosmology. Philosophic theory that treats of the ultimate character of the universe.

Empathy. In connection with a response to human beings, a tendency to "feel with" another; to place oneself in the position of another and to experience what the other experiences.

Empiricism. The philosophical view that experience is the only source of knowledge, a view contrasting with nativism and a priorism.

Epicritic sensation or sensibility. One of two divisions (the other is the protopathic system) of cutaneous sensing: it is responsive to light touch, warmth, and coolth, but not to pain or extremes of temperature sensed as such; localization is very delicate.

Ethnocentrism. The tendency to exalt the superiority of the group (especially the national or ethnic group) to which one belongs and to judge outsiders, often contemptuously, by the standards of one's own group.

Extraversion. 1. Literally, a turning outward. 2. An attitude of interest in things outside oneself, in the physical and social environment, rather than in one's own thoughts and feelings.

Gestalt psychology or theory. The systematic position that psychological phenomena are organized, undivided, articulated wholes or gestalts. The

* Most definitions are abridged from H. B. English and A. C. English, *A Comprehensive Dictionary of Psychological and Psychoanalytic Terms.* New York: Longmans, Green and Co., Inc., 1958.

properties of a gestalt are properties of the whole as such and are not derived by summation of its parts. Conversely, the parts derive their properties from their membership in the whole.

Identification. Most frequently, in connection with personality development, the process of seeing another person as an extension of oneself, hence seeking satisfactions through that other, and sharing the other's griefs and triumphs.

Idiographic. Pertaining to, or characterizing, an account of a particular case or of individual cases or events.

Imageless thought. (Structural psychology) an idea or thought which, upon careful introspective analysis, reveals no sensations or images.

Imagery. 1. The imagining processes taken collectively; or the process of imagining, in general. 2. The kind of mental images characteristically used in a particular kind of task, or by an individual.

Intuition. 1. Direct and apparently unmediated knowledge. Used sometimes in connection with sense knowledge, since no cogitation is involved; and of any other directly received knowledge. 2. A judgment, meaning, or idea that occurs to a person without any known process of cogitation or reflective thinking.

Intervening variable or I.V. 1. Any variable that is functionally connected with a preceding and a following variable. 2. More restrictedly, the expression in condensed form of the relationship between the control conditions and the dependent variable. Gravitation is not an entity and not a cause; it is an I.V.; it has no meaning other than the series of quantitative relationships that describe the reciprocal movements toward each other of bodies having mass.

Ipsative. Focusing on a single individual as in ipsative scaling, a method of assigning scale values with the individual's own characteristic behavior as the standard of comparison.

Law or principle of effect. An empirical generalization that an organism learns more quickly those reactions that are accompanied or followed by a satisfying state of affairs, and learns slowly or not at all those that result in an annoying state of affairs.

Median or Md(n). 1. The value (attained by calculation) that separates into halves all the cases in a ranked distribution. 2. That score in a ranked distribution which has exactly half of the cases below it and half (or half minus one, when N is an even number) above it.

Morphogenesis. The origin and development of form or structure in an organism.

Nomothetic. Characterizing procedures and methods designed to discover general laws. Contrasted with idiographic, which pertains to the attempt to understand a particular event or individual.

Normative. Pertaining to norms, standards, or values; emphasizing comparisons among individuals.

Perception. 1. An event in the person or organism, primarily cognitive but also controlled by the excitation of sensory receptors, bearing on the recognition or organization of external objects or events. 2. The awareness, or the process of becoming aware, of extraorganic or intraorganic objects or relations or qualities, by means of sensory processes and under the influence of set and of prior experiences.

Positivism. 1. The philosophical point of view, formulated by Comte, which sought to dispense with all theological and metaphysical concepts. 2. The doctrine that science is limited to observed facts and to what can be rigorously deduced from facts, that all concepts and conclusions refer to facts and derive all their meaning from facts.

Primary drive. A drive which in its major form is determined by the animal's heredity; a drive that depends upon a physiological need and that, independent of prior learning, instigates a special class of behavior.

Projection. 1. The process of unwittingly attributing one's own traits, attitudes, or subjective processes to others: e.g., the child's naive assumption that adults feel as he does. 2. The process of ascribing to others one's own unacknowledged desires or faults. This is presumed to be a defense against a sense of guilt or inadequacy.

Protopathic sensations. The genetically older of two divisions of cutaneous sensing; a system in which there is only gross localization or other discrimination, but extremes of temperature are sensed as such and there is ready susceptibility to pain.

Psychoanalysis. A body of doctrine set forth by Freud, with modifications by his close disciples. The doctrine is based on the concepts of unconscious motivation, conflict, and symbolism. The boundaries of psychoanalysis are not sharply defined.

Psychodynamic. Characterizing any psychological system that strives for explanation of behavior in terms of motives or drives; of a system that attributes causal efficiency to certain (or to all) psychological processes.

Psychopathology. The systematic investigation of morbid mental conditions. Strictly speaking, psychopathology is a branch of psychological science and is to be contrasted with clinical psychology and psychiatry, which are technology.

Psychosis. Any severe, specific mental disorder or disease process that has a characteristic origin, course, and symptoms.

Psychotic. Pertaining to a psychotic disorder or psychosis; characterizing a certain behavior pattern as symptomatic of psychotic disorder or (at least) as strongly resembling the behavior of such a disorder.

Recipathy. A term formed by combining *reciprocal* and *sympathy* to mean an interaction at the level of feeling such that two persons, from sharing each other's feelings, come to a common feeling.

Reliability. In the area of measurement, the complex property of a series of observations, of a measuring instrument, or of the entire measuring process, that makes possible the obtaining of similar results upon repetition; the degree to which such similar results may be predicted; the degree to which measurement is free from random influence.

Repression. The exclusion of specific psychological activities or contents from conscious awareness by a process of which the individual is not directly aware. Exclusion includes preventing entry into, forcing out of, or continuously preventing return to, consciousness.

Response set. A readiness to respond; an "openness" to stimulation.

Retroactive inhibition. Impairment of the normal effects of a learning activity when it is followed closely by another activity, especially one somewhat similar to the first; or the hypothetical process accountable therefor.

Schizophrenia or schizophrenic reaction. A group of psychotic reactions characterized by fundamental disturbances in reality relationships, by a conceptual world determined excessively by feeling, and by marked affective, intellectual, and overt behavioral disturbances.

Secondary drive. A drive aroused and/or satisfied in ways acquired by experience or learning; a drive that is not a part of the species-specific repertory of an animal.

Sensory. 1. Pertaining to the activity of a sense organ. 2. Pertaining to directly observed objective data, i.e., to sense data.

Sensory-motor or sensorimotor. 1. Pertaining to the neural transit from a sense organ to a muscle. Some authors use the form sensory-motor and restrict it to this meaning. 2. Descriptive of any act whose nature is primarily dependent upon the combined or integrated functioning of sense organs and motor mechanisms.

Set. *See* Response set.

Structuralistic introspectionism or structural psychology. A point of view or school of psychology that analyzes mental states or contents into elementary constituents by the method of introspection aided by experiment.

Valence. (K. Lewin) that property of an object or region in the life space by virtue of which the object is sought (positive valence) or avoided (negative valence).

Variable. A quantity that may increase or decrease, continuously or discontinuously, without other essential change: e.g., the area of skin stimulated, the intensity of the stimulus, the number of correct answers on a test, the time taken to react. In psychology, three classes of variables are distinguished: R variables, responses or acts; S variables, properties of the physical or social environment; O variables, the organic or organismic or personal variables, the changeable properties of the person or organism. The R variable is always the dependent variable.

VTE or vicarious trial and error. (K. Muenzinger) the substitution of a mental performance for an overt performance in the tentative behaviors designed to solve a problem; the substitution of imagined responses for the overt in the tryouts of problem-solving.